Twilight Inventory

A Collection of Forgotten 8-Bit

Adventure Games

By Gareth Pitchford

www.8bitAG.com

ISBN: 978-0-244-35119-9

(Printed Version)

Versions of many of the reviews and articles in this book originally appeared in Adventure Probe, Red Herring, From Beyond, and the Sam Coupe Adventure Club magazine.

Contents

Introduction

In 1980s Britain, the personal computer was king when it came to home gaming. Shielded from the crash that hit the US video game industry, the UK market was the birthplace of, what seemed at the time like an endless conveyor belt of different 8-bit "micros". Machines like Sinclair's ZX81 and ZX Spectrum, Amstrad's CPC and PCW, Acorn's Electron and BBC Micro, rubbed shoulders with less-commercially successful entries such as the Oric and Dragon. Even the almighty American challengers, the Commodore Vic-20 and C64 struggled to dominate this vast, vibrantly haphazard marketplace.

These home computers could never truly replicate the experience of arcade gaming or compete with the focused power of the Japanese gaming consoles that arrived on the scene much later, not that they didn't give it a good go. However, there was one genre that they truly excelled at... the humble text adventure.

For the text adventure, flashy graphics were optional and a decent keyboard (or, even, one made of rubber) was the perfect input device. You simply plugged your home computer into your television set, fired up your cassette player or disk drive and you had access to a whole world of imaginative, creative and unique gaming experiences.

Inspired by American text adventure legends such as Crowther & Woods, Infocom, and Scott Adams, the UK produced its own big-hitters. Names such as Magnetic Scrolls, Level 9, Delta 4 and Brian Howarth became synonymous with the early adventure scene and created titles that were just as highly regarded by their native audience.

It wasn't just big, commercial companies that produced text adventures. One of the attractions about the genre was that virtually anyone could produce their own, playable game.

Early homegrown efforts, often programmed in BASIC, were usually slow and struggled to understand the commands that players typed in, but many talented programmers went on to produce their own 'machine-coded' games that were much more impressive.

The real breakthrough, in terms of homegrown adventures, came with the release of two pieces of software; Incentive's Graphic Adventure Creator and Gilsoft's The Quill. Followed a few years later by The Professional Adventure Writer, these were complete adventure writing systems. These programs took care of almost all the technical aspects of producing an adventure. They provided an adventure creator with a working parser, a framework for the game locations and a format for easily adding in puzzles. And, more importantly, they granted authors the rights to publish the games they made without paying Incentive or Gilsoft a royalty.

These adventure writing systems allowed consumers of the media to very easily become creators; making games for family and friends, and also, with very little extra effort, the wider public.

Graphics, never a huge draw for the true devotee of the text adventure, were optional (as was often the ability to spell). To produce your own game the only thing you really had to be able to do was to type basic descriptions and come up with ideas for puzzles.

For a short time, even homebrewed efforts were considered good enough for commercial release. Big publishers such as Firebird, Alternative Software, Mirrorsoft, CRL, Automata, and Games Workshop all released games produced using the GAC and the Quill. The text adventure's time in the sun was relatively short-lived, however, as software houses soon felt their audience wanted more graphical, arcade-inspired experiences.

But even before the big publishers believed that their audience had tired and moved on from text adventures, a whole cottage industry of homegrown software houses had sprung up.

In a market that had grown initially from the sales of tape cassettes stuffed into jiffy bags or software sold at 'microfairs', there had always been a very thin diving line between the professional publisher and hobbyist. Sending off for games by post wasn't an alien or new concept.

Reaching and growing their audience, through easily accessible channels such as Mike Gerrard's Your Sinclair column, adventure authors took on the role of publishers themselves. Cheques and postal orders were traded for photocopied inlays and hand-duplicated cassette tapes. A thriving cottage industry blossomed.

What were these homebrewed adventures like? Although there was a steady stream of games set in schools and a whole host of parodies of The Hobbit and Star Wars, the homegrown community also crafted a collection of unique, novel experiences. Taking inspiration from folklore, legends, films and books, these were games with stories and settings unvisited in mainstream titles both back then and now.

Zenobi Software, undoubtedly the largest and most successful homegrown company on any format, was built on the sales of founder John Wilson's own Tolkien-parodying adventures. It wasn't long before he'd moved on to publishing the work of other authors, getting a reputation not just for the professional way he dealt with customers but also for his generous royalty rate for authors.

Fanzines sprang up to support the scene that was increasingly being overlooked by the mainstream magazines. Titles such as the long-running Adventure Probe, From Beyond, Red Herring, Spellbreaker, and Adventure Coder were written and produced by both the players and the writers active in the community at the time. Readers of Adventure Probe even organised an annual UK convention for lovers of the genre.

There are several books available that discuss the heydays of 8-bit adventure gaming, the time when such games were considered commercially viable, but very few that document the twilight years.

This book collects together reviews and articles I wrote for various adventure game fanzines back in the early 1990s.

Presented here, largely unedited they hopefully form a snapshot of the small, but vibrant UK 8-bit adventure game scene at that time.

The material in this book largely focuses on games created for the ZX Spectrum range of computers but several titles converted from other formats, such as the Amstrad CPC and Commodore 64, are also discussed.

Interspersed between the reviews are snippets of background information about many of the creators. I hope you will find the information useful. I've also included a large collection of shorter reviews and game synopses.

My thanks go to the authors of these adventures who provided me with many hours of entertainment and who I can blame, in part, for distracting me from my GCSEs, A-Levels and degree. Many apologies if I was too harsh on your games in my reviews. Please take solace from the fact that my own efforts at homegrown adventure writing also generated a range of mixed reactions!

Adventure Game Reviews

Agatha's Folly (Spectrum 48K)

by Linda Wright

Published by Marlin Games / Zenobi Software

Mention Linda Wright to any seasoned adventurer and you're likely to be swamped in a sea of praise for her games. And it's praise that's well deserved. Her games are renowned for their quality, devious puzzles and Linda Wright shine. 'Agatha's Folly' is no exception.

Anyway, enough of that waffle. 'Agatha's Folly' is a two-part PAWed game with a plot that goes something like this...

You've just become the proud owner of a country cottage – Something you have been dreaming of buying for years. Mind you, it's not quite what you expected, but with a little lick of paint and a bit of re-arranging it'll do you. Exploring the grounds, you were surprised to see that you'd also acquired a small lake, a semi-derelict mill and a 'folly' with the property. The 'folly' gave you a strange feeling, a very strange feeling.

Never mind, you've got no time for that. Although your furniture won't arrive until tomorrow you've decided to spend the night at the cottage. It'll give you a good chance to explore – And who knows, maybe you can find out some more about the previous owner of the cottage, a certain Agatha, who was said to have mysteriously vanished!

Once the game starts you've plenty to do. The house needs a bit of exploring, but with the continual interruptions of people at the door you'll be lucky if you get chance. Mind you, they're very helpful and you get some snippets of information off them about Agatha.

Linda was always very good at hiding objects, and this game's no exception. You really do have to examine everything in sight and use a hell of a lot of logical thinking in places.

Before too long, you'll find out that Agatha was obsessed with UFOs and men from outer space, maybe the Folly's something to do with that? Mind you, there's no way of telling until you manage to find some way across the lake.

Once you've sussed out this part you'll move onto the next bit, which is a different kettle of fish. The tempo changes and you're into a game that contrasts with the first but still has the same stylish, polished approach.

'Agatha's Folly' is not a game that you'll solve in an evening. It's one with plenty of problems that'll keep you burning the old lamps for many an hour.

```
THE ENTRANCE HALL.
Glancing around at the peeling
plaster and grubby paint you
begin to wonder if you'll ever
have the time to make this place
look habitable. Even the stairs
are covered in grime, and the
rug on the floor is filthy.
Exit(s): S.E.W.N.U.

>EXAMINE RUG
OK, but you see nothing special.

>EXAMINE STAIRS
Checking the stairway, you
notice a cupboard that you
hadn't seen before.


>OPEN CUPBOARD
```

Having started her adventuring career writing the Amstrad CPC titles 'Sharpe's Deeds' and 'The Black Fountain' for mainstream publisher Incentive Software, Linda Wright moved to the Spectrum to produce adventures for her own Marlin Games label. 'Agatha's Folly', 'The Beast', 'The Jade Stone' and 'Cloud 99' were highly regarded and went on to be re-released by Zenobi Software.

Al-Strad (Spectrum 48K)

by Paul Gill

Published by The Guild

'Al-Strad' is one of the many adventures that The Guild have transferred between various formats. It originally started out its life as a game written in BASIC and machine code on the Commodore 64.

The 'plot' is as follows. In the far-off kingdom of Megabyte there lived a King called Kilobyte. All was happy and peaceful in this rather strange land until the evil SINK kidnapped King Kilobyte's daughter Sally Software. You are Al-Strad and must rescue Sally from the evil SINK's LAIR.

The game's Amstrad roots show up in the Spectrum version. It is very much a return to the more traditional problems of adventuring. You start off being hungry for instance. There's the usual river to be crossed, a dog to get passed, a crocodile to get rid of as well as the mazes (which come in the form of the forest of deja-vu and the puckman maze). Does that mean that the adventure is lacking in originality?

```
You are inside the huge oak.
It's very small and cramped and
it smells awful (stupid
squirrels...)

Visible exits:- out.

You can also see
a pair of armbands.

You are hungry!

What next?
*GET ARMBANDS

You now have the pair of
armbands.

You are hungry!

What now?
*
```

The answer is No. For the world of Megabyte is hardly dull – In fact it's totally wacky. At points in the game you'll find yourself flying, taking a space rocket to the moon, and giving a computer game to someone so that they melt(?). You also come across several well-known computer characters – There's even a bloke called Kevin Tons of Adductive (Remember him??)

The game features all the usual commands you'd expect in a PAWed game as well as QSAVE, QLOAD, AGAIN and EXITS. It's also a lot better put together than some of the other Guild conversions – It makes you feel as though Pegasus Software have taken their time with the game transfer.

To sum it all up, Al-Strad is a mildly humorous game with 'Quill'-type puzzles. A few of you may not like it because of its sudden changes in locations and lateral, pun-type problems, but at £2 it's worth checking out.

Paul Gill's Al-Strad started life as a Commodore 64 adventure before being converted to the Amstrad (by Rhinosoft) and the Spectrum (by The Guild). He also wrote the Amstrad game, 'Die You Vicious Fish'.

Amulet of Darath (Spectrum 48K)

by Macsoft (Mark Walker)

Published by Zenobi Software

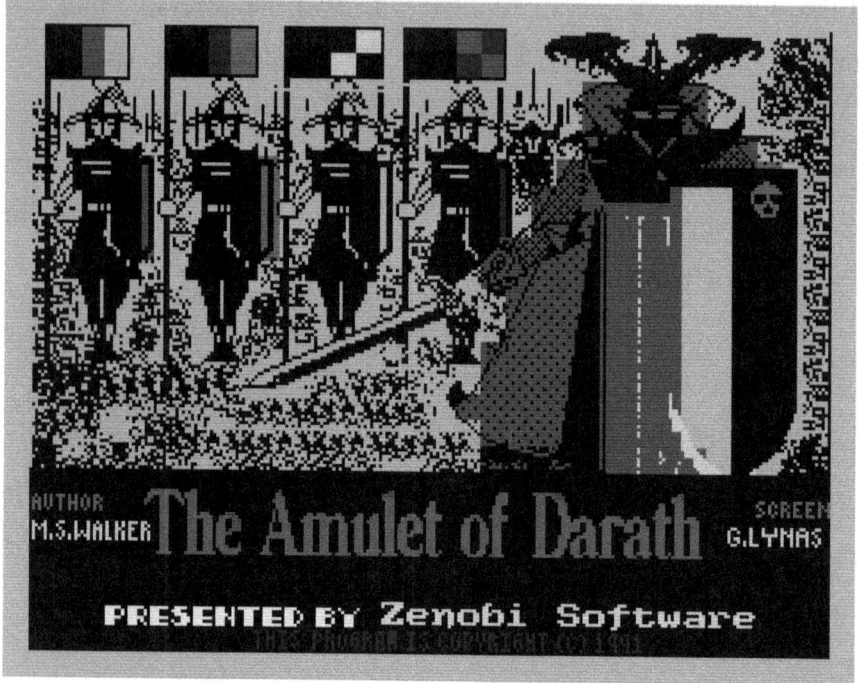

The King of Erutnevda has apparently sent me on a quest to save the land from the evil Lord Paralax. I seemed to be a character called Zachra and had to find the two pieces of the Amulet to complete the game. Nothing amazing in the plot, I thought, but let's get down to the adventure proper.

I started in the local pub. The landlord tried to rip me off by charging me 1 copper coin for a measly mug of mead, but I ignored this. After all, he let me walk out of his tavern with the mug so I could hardly have complained, could I?

It appeared that I could have the screen displayed in various modes. BRIEF text mode merely printed up the name of the location, while VERBOSE printed up the full location description. It wasn't long before I had realised that there wasn't much difference between the two. Then there was the command EXITS on/off to, yes, you guessed it, turn the exit display line on or off.

```
 Outside the Inn. It is a muddy,
much-used road. The smell of
stale ale comes from inside the
inn. Also here is a pile of
leaves.

Exits: S W.

>EXAMINE LEAVES
The leaves are brown and dry.

>SEARCH LEAVES
Searching amongst the leaves,
Zachra finds an old glove.

>EXAMINE GLOVE
The glove is made of leather.

>I
```

Pretty soon I had found out that SEARCH was very useful. On occasions it was even a good idea to REMOVE things from their resting places. I had also tested out the spells. I had been given three of them, and they could each be used only once. With cryptic names like DEATH, SHIFT and FIRE I just had to test them out to see what they did.

There didn't appear to be many locations to explore. There were also a few sudden deaths. In no time at all, I had been killed by soldiers, poisoned food and other things and was getting rather brassed off.

The parser wasn't helping matters. The game wasn't that hard, but was made harder by the pedantic programmer. Take for instance the task of making some magical paste out of some water and some granules. The water has to be collected in a mug (which, by the way, you can't DROP because, and I quote, 'you haven't got that'). The thing is that there are several locations with water in, but the program only allows you to get the water from one location. And you have to GET WATER, the more usual FILL MUG WITH WATER doesn't work.

Once I had the water, I needed to get at the granules. EXAMining the bottle showed it to be tightly stoppered shut. So I typed OPEN BOTTLE. 'It won't budge'. Ok, then. SMASH BOTTLE. 'You can't do that'. Various other things were tried and the answer was found to be the rather obscure UNSTOPPER BOTTLE – After which I was told that I had pulled the cork from the bottle.

So, I'd got the granules, right? No. As soon as I UNSTOPPERed the bottle a freak gust of wind blew the granules (from inside the bottle?!?!) away. This was while I was inside a sheltered room. The thing is that the programmer only allows you to open the bottle in the room where the granules are to be used rather than letting you OPEN the bottle somewhere else and then EMPTY it in the location where you make the paste. Stupid!

A lot of the game is like that. It has lots of cop-out responses, illogical puzzles and a damned annoying parser. I really did want to enjoy this game but each time that I felt myself getting somewhere I was stopped short by a short-sighted programming hitch.

```
 Sleeping Quarters. The Tyrant
Lord cares greatly for his
soldiers, as the quarters are
large and well-furnished. The
bed which Zachra is standing
next to is small, with a lumpy
mattress. Also here is a bed.

Exits: E W.


>EXAMINE BED
The bed is quite comfortable,
but the mattress is lumpy.


>LIFT MATTRESS
Zachra lifts the mattress and
underneath, he finds a pass.

>GET PASS
```

Amulet of Darath is not an awful game but it could have been so much better if it'd been more user-friendly.

The Antillis Mission (Spectrum 48K)

By Jon Lemmon

Published by Compass Software

'Antillis' is a game that's reminiscent of the old TV series 'Voyage to The Bottom of The Sea' and, in a way, even 'Star Trek'! You take on the role of Captain Alan Henson, an underwater trouble-shooter, and you must figure out just what has gone wrong with the ZX3.

The ZX3 is not a forerunner to the ZX81 (or, in fact, anything to do with Sir Clive) but rather an experimental nuclear submarine. The ZX3 has malfunctioned and is at a depth of some 14 miles under the surface. The most alarming thing is that the android crew appear to have malfunctioned as well, and, as there are forty nuclear missiles on board, that's not an ideal thing to happen! The cause could be the mysterious neutron ray that as bombarding the sub, and the solution... well, that's your job.

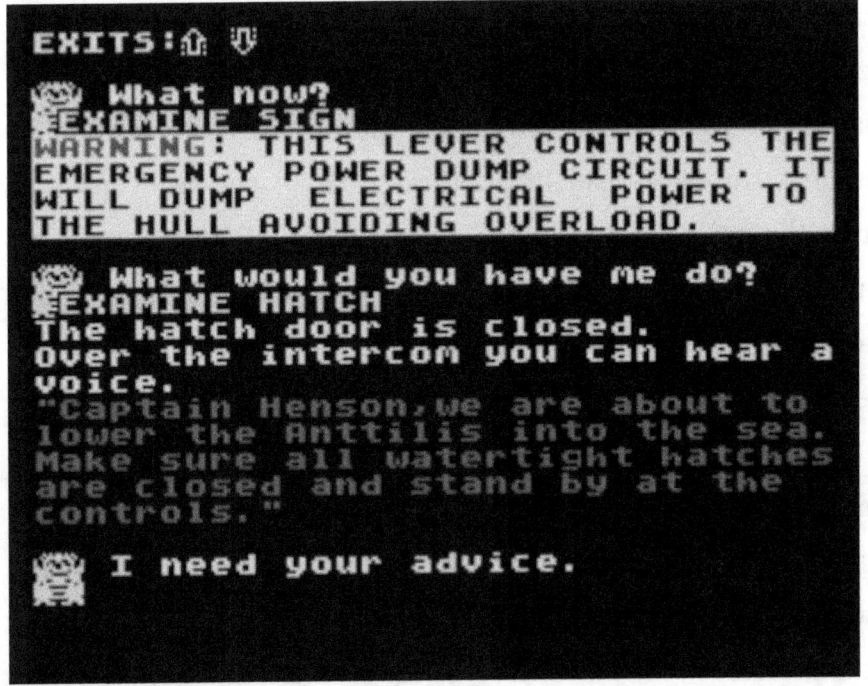

You start alongside your mini-sub, the Antillis, where you'll receive some information about the task ahead. Once inside you'll have time to explore the ship (and note the radiation decontamination compartment, the controls and the weird lever that you shouldn't pull until right at the end of the game or you'll feel your spirits crushed!) before the first task displays itself... someone has tampered with the craft's autopilot so you have to find a way of getting that back online, so you can actually get to the ZX3.

The solution lies in a handy little gadget that poses as a scanner. This scanner houses a small, but powerful, little computer that will enable you to do a variety of different tasks. The scanner activates the Compass VIP (Visual Information Panel) system and displays things like your current radiation level (don't let it get too high or you'll die) and the scanners battery power (keep topping it up, without the scanner you'll be useless, trapped, dead or all three). These panels drop down from the top of the screen like the menus on a WIMP system and are a nice little feature. You can also use your scanner to open doors, ask for computer assistance, disarm the missiles and reprogram any androids that you may encounter.

Your main tasks on your mission are to neutralise all the malfunctioning androids, disarm as many nuclear missiles as you can and get the subs main computer functional again. Sounds easy? It's not! You have to be constantly watching your radiation level, the power level of the scanner, and hopping from task to task dealing with androids and other obstacles on the way. It's all very hectic, and more like a strategy game than a conventional adventure, but it's great fun.

The game has the usual Compass polish and screen/sound FXs. Though a tad short on the more usual adventuring problems this is more than made up for by the strategy element. I've always liked the way that Compass Software and Jon Lemmon are constantly trying to explore new possibilities of adventuring elements from within PAW... work that seems not to be appreciated by a large number of adventurers.

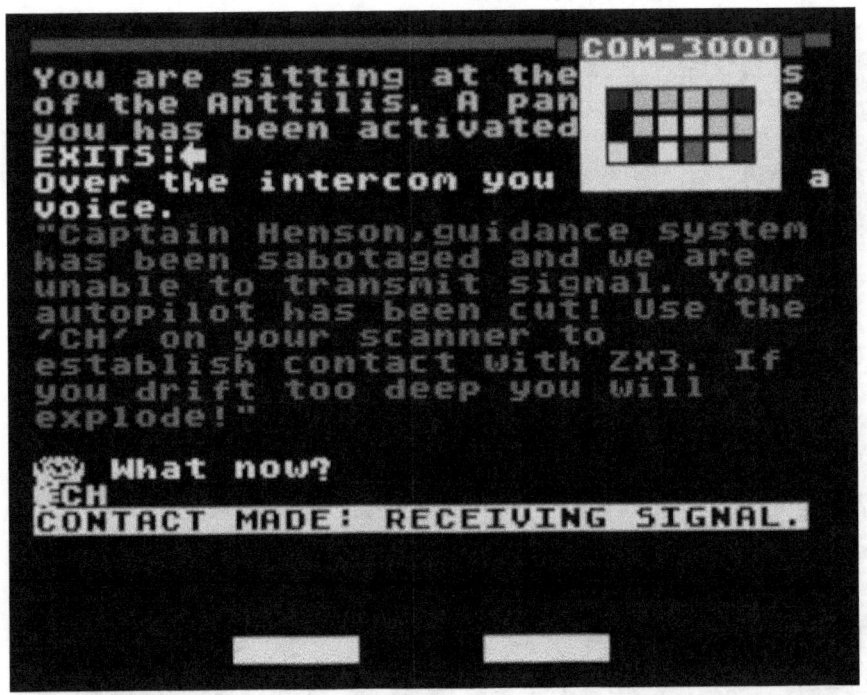

Overall, a compulsive adventure game with more than a spoonful of strategy. Well worth checking out if you like something different, but if you prefer conventional GET object/USE object adventures you may be disappointed.

Arnold the Adventurer II (Spectrum 48K)

By Scott Denyer

Published by Zenobi Software

```
What next?
>EXAMINE BED
It serves its purpose.

What now?
>EXAMINE TABLE
A table that bears a strange
resemblance to something called
a table.

What should Arnold do now?
>EXAMINE CHAIR
Despite large spending, this was
an old chair that looked like it
would collapse at any moment.

What next?
>SIT ON CHAIR
Arnold placed his plump behind
on the chair, and as he did so
one of the legs snapped off...
```

'The prat with the cape is back', is the self-deprecating sub-title of 'Arnold 2'. The game follows on from the original game, 'Arnold the Adventurer' and features the same main character. It's a good idea to play the original first – a fact which publisher John Wilson must have realised as he's cunningly included Arnold I on the other side of the tape. So, what's the plot then?

Since destroying the evil Swartze and saving the land, Arnold Tanglewood had become a national hero. But fame, unfortunately, doesn't last long and that was the case with Arnold. However, the chance of a sequel was always a possibility and indeed that's what happened. For the skies grew dark and an evil atmosphere crept across the land again. Winthorpe the Wizard thought he had found the source of the darkness, but he had disappeared. Arnold didn't know what the source was, but he knew that something would turn up in the end. It was not long before the people called upon Arnold once again and asked him to search out and destroy the evil menace. And that's where the story really starts...

You begin the game in Arnie's house, with his newly acquired furniture dotted around. It doesn't appear very stable though, as you soon find out when you attempt to sit on some of it. Oh well, at least the garden's blooming.

Down the road, Schwartze's old mansion is crumbling away, while in the other direction you'll meet a lot of old friends. This is why it's best to play (and complete?) the original first, as if you don't then you won't get half of the in-jokes and references to Arnold's previous outing.

It's not very long before you come across some problems. A farmer's cart blocks the entrance to the barn and you can't move it because it hasn't got all four wheels. Elsewhere, a fisherman blocks your way until you can give him something fishy and an old woman does the same 'til you find her a spoon (a spoon??). Even more problems lie across the lake, on an island, though make sure you finish all the ones on the mainland first!

Old Tharg, the wolf, is here again. But you'll have to rescue him before he's of any use, as he's in a dog kennel! The boatman is back, but don't try to wake him this time – He won't give you two chances like in the original.

The text is in usual Denyer 'laid-back' style. There are plenty of puzzles, though many are simplistic, and it should keep you busy for a while. (Certainly longer than the original game!)

Apart from a stab at yours truly in a hidden message, and a few occasions where the parser wasn't quite as friendly as it ought to have been, I can't find much to fault. Maybe there were too many references to the original game, which would have been disastrous had the original not been given away with it, but then that's all part of the fun and a real buzz for the people who have played, and enjoyed, the earlier title.

Overall, not Scott Denyer's best game but a funny and playable game all the same. Worth getting.

Arnold the Adventurer III (Spectrum 48K)

By Scott Denyer

Published by Zenobi Software

```
Arnold stood in Winthorpe's old
shack. The sun beamed through
the hole in the wall that should
have housed a window, but
didn't. Shelves were stacked
with rows upon rows of books,
while on the table in the centre
of the room stood a large
cauldron. A cupboard stood on
one wall also. The door leads
north.
Arnold could also see...
Winthorpe the wizard, lying in
bed, moaning.

What now?
>EXAMINE WINTHORPE
Winthorpe is rather green, and
he is covered in red blotches.

What next, Arnold?
>_
```

The world's most unlikely super-hero Arnold Tanglewood
is back in his third adventure 'Arnold the Adventurer III – This
time it's personal'.

Arnold's task this time reared its head when he went to
visit his old pal Winthorpe who had picked up a few walk-on
parts in Arnie's previous adventures. Arriving at Winthorpe's
'digs' in the middle of Fancy Forest (the in-place for Wizards to
be seen) he was distressed to find his favourite magic wielder in
a very sorry state, covered from head to toe in unsightly

blotches... What has happened to Winthorpe? Is he auditioning for the part of Mr Blobby? It's up to you to find out.

This is where the game opens and as usual you play Arnold. Finding out what's wrong with Winny isn't all that difficult – the nice orange instruction sheet Zenobi supplies with the game tells you all – but upon looking round the interior of Win's shack your worst fears are confirmed when you come across a book on magical diseases and find out that Winthorpe has caught 'Wizarditis'. Serves him right really, he knows how dangerous magic can be and yet he still insists on doing it without adequate protection (old Winny's not one for pointed hats and robes!). It seems that only the fabled Goblett Of Goodness can save him... but that lies in the land of the flower-people; you'd have to be mad to go there!

But you are mad, you're Arnold remember, and so off you go into the depths of the forest after having a quick shufty round Winthorpe's shack and remembering that Scott can be as bad as Larry Horsfield when it comes to making you LOOK UNDER things. The number of locations you can initially visit is very limited and the problems are tricky from the word go.

Still, once you've used your nut to get past the wolf and helped a fog with haemorrhoids you'll be getting more into the swing of things. The hamlet of Gerbilsbury lies nearby with its own little market and plenty of Scott's favourite vegetables. In fact the vegetable store has a crisis on its hands... the owner was operating a 'vegetable swap scheme' – the only problem was that everybody gave him cabbages in exchange for more interesting greens and now cabbages are the only thing he's got on the stall.

```
Arnold was on a bracken-covered
path leading through the forest.
To the west, the path opened out
into the sunlight of a small
clearing, while it also led east
into even darker forest.
Arnold could also see...
A sinister wolfhound, drooling
and baring its fangs.
═══════════════════════════════════

What should Arnold do now?
≥EXAMINE WOLFHOUND
"Nothing particularly
outstanding about that!"
observed Arnold.

The wolfhound reared, and then
threw itself at Arnold's throat.
Without even time to say "Fangs
for the memory!", Arnold died...
                              ➡
```

Elsewhere you'll come across some men playing bowls and the world famous Balrog Brothers. If you can help the Balrogs then you'll be better off... just don't take things too far!

The text is the usual Scotty D. fare –cheerful and bubbly. Scott's games, particularly the Arnold ones, have always reminded me of John Wilson's adventures and Arnold III is no exception... it could just have easily been a 'Bulbo' title.

I must admit that I had some awful problems with the parser – and with the game puzzles being difficult (and sometimes just flippin' obscure) this tended to show up the little glitches all the more. Even the simple things were sometimes difficult – getting through a window couldn't be achieved by the usual CLIMB THROUGH WINDOW or GO WINDOW but only by CLIMB IN. A lot of things, like the hole or the tree-stump, just produce the standard EXAMINE message when a little hint, or even a mere acknowledgement that the object in question was important or relevant would have been appreciated.

Overall though, Arnold III is quite fun but not a beginner's game... which is a bit of a shame as I normally recommend Arnold I as a good title to start out with. If you like Scott's 'teenage' humour and tricky puzzles then this one should be right up your street.

Aztec Assault (Spectrum 48K)

Written by The Traveller in Black (Ian S. Brown)

Published by Zenobi Software

After reviewing 'The Violator of Voodoo' I was eagerly awaiting the next game in the Phoenix series... and here it is. But is it as good as the last?

The answer is a resounding yes, once again the Traveller has successfully combined an era in time with the Phoenix format. This time it's 1519 A.D....

As Phoenix you find yourself in the very heart of the Aztec empire... at Tenochtitlan itself. The 'Primal Darkness's handiwork is in clear evidence as you wander around. An early meeting with an Aztec priest brings you up to date. Demons roam the religious centres and the ashes of the past leaders have disappeared. To top it all, the snake-woman Cuicoatl appears transformed and possibly possessed. Not that Cuicoatl is a nice sight anyway, he (yes, he is a he despite his name) has two serpents as heads, a necklace of human hearts and claws on his hands and his feet.

Because of the demon invasion, human sacrifices cannot be carried out. You may think that that's a good thing but according to the Aztecs, stopping the sacrifices will anger the gods and bring about the 5th Sun. Earthquakes will devastate the Earth and the Apocalypse will take place causing the monsters of the twilight, the Tzutzimime, to swarm out and hurl themselves on the survivors. It is clear that the Abomination must be stopped or the whole planet may be in danger.

So, you journey further into the city. An Aztec family stand on the edge of Lake Texcoco waiting for the body of their son to surface so that they may bury him. As in the previous two games good deeds always pay off and helping this family, and the man you encounter in the baths will enable you to get that little bit further.

You also help with a pregnancy! The object required is a little strange, but it's all in keeping with the Aztec scenario. Like the previous game, 'The Violator of Voodoo', the adventure has been thoroughly researched and is 100% accurate in regards to what we know about the culture and traditions of the Aztec people.

Actually getting into the religious city itself may give you some difficulties as the defence bridges have been removed making it impossible to cross by normal means. However, a careful EXAMination will reveal an alternate method of travel.

You'll eventually meet up with the snake-woman, surrounded by guards and a red demon. The snake-woman says, "So you are the Phoenix who defeated the Abomination. You won't defeat me, insect". Indeed, it will take a lot to rid the city of the minions of the 'Primal Darkness'... an awful lot.

Summing up. Another great game in the 'Phoenix' series. Carefully crafted, thoroughly researched, and well-programmed. Worth checking out.

The Base (Amstrad CP/M+)

Written by Ken Bond

Published by The Guild

Ken Bond's Amstrad adventures are well praised by adventurers, and looking at 'The Base' it is easy to see just why.

'The Base' starts with you waking up from a dream in which you thought you were being chased. You find yourself in a locked cell with just a bed (complete with bed-pan) and a window visible. At this point in the game you have absolutely no idea who you are or what your task is... but it doesn't take a genius to have a good guess. Yes, that's right, the idea is to escape.

But how? There's nothing much in the room that will help. After a few moves, however, someone pushes a package through the window and upon opening it you discover that inside is a brass key... the key to the cell? But you shouldn't use it yet. Taking a closer look at the packaging you see that there's a message written inside telling you to wait until it's safe before you venture outside. Sure enough, after you wait for a few moves, you hear the snoring of the guard. When you unlock and leave the cell you discover that the same person who pushed the package through the bars of your cell appears to have drugged your jailor. You must move fast before he wakes up.

You can now move around the prison, but watch out for

the guards. Various locked doors block your way, but you are eventually able to get through a few of them. You discover rooms like the mortuary and the execution chamber... not very nice places. Then you manage to get into the Governor's office (it is night time) where you find his safe. Elsewhere in the prison offices you find a telex that reveals that you are a spy, captured by the prison officers yesterday. Your mission was to capture the plans of a submarine being built at Viccio... this will now be your target, once you escape.

Elsewhere a useful lift allows access to other parts of the Base. The Governor's apartment is luxurious and you tip-toe around, careful not to wake the Governor and his wife in bed, in the hope of finding some useful objects. You discover a blank cassette tape but decide not to play it in the nearby hi-fi in fear of waking your captors... you reckon that you'll soon find somewhere else to use it.

And so, you'll continue moving round the base, getting that little bit further each time until eventually you'll move onto the second load where you're after the plans to the submarine.

The game is full of locations... everything that you would expect in a real base is here – from a surgery and a gymnasium, to toilets and bathrooms. Ken has included a hell of a lot of puzzles which will keep you scratching your head for a long time.

There are a few text errors... in the CP/M Public Domain version at least, but then that is only to be expected (though not necessarily excused). On the whole, though, it's a well presented and very playable game that is well worth getting hold of.

```
The Cell. You are in a small
cell about 6 feet wide by 12
feet long. An iron bed is
against the north wall under a
small barred window high up in
the stone wall. The only other
object in the cell besides
yourself is a metal chamber pot
under the bed. A metal door with
a small peephole covered on the
outside is to the south.

∞∞∞∞∞∞∞∞∞∞∞∞∞∞∞∞∞∞∞∞∞∞∞∞∞∞∞∞∞∞∞∞∞∞∞∞

What should you do now?
$EXAMINE DOOR
It is made of very strong metal.
The keyhole has a brass
surround.

What should you do next?
$/
```

In addition to CP/M+ versions being compatible with the Spectrum +3 (running the associated DOS), Amstrad-based author Ken Bond also had several of his games converted to Spectrum; 'The Test', 'The Island', 'Castle Warlock' and 'The Spiro Legacy'.

The Beginning of the End (Spectrum 48K)

Written by Jonathan Scott

Published by Zenobi Software

```
►►►►►  The Beginning of the End ►►►►►
Here I am in a spacious
classroom which holds five rows
of desks, with one separate from
the rest, beside a careworn
cupboard below a window in the
east wall. On the wall is a
mediocre wallclock (best place
for it!).

Exit(s): none.
»EXAMINE DESK
Nothing seems to be on top of
it.
»EXAMINE UNDER DESK
Under the desk, there's an
airtight container!
»EXAMINE CONTAINER
It is closed.
»OPEN CONTAINER«
```

Not having played any of the earlier games in the Zikov Trilogy ('Red Alert' and 'Escape From Hodgkins' Manor') I wasn't quite sure what to expect from this game. Barbara Gibb, the game's playtester, told me that it was definitely difficult but that I should enjoy it... The author apparently has an off-beat sense of humour that she thought might be akin to mine. I don't know what she means, I mean I may have had a few giant coffee machines and strange woolly jumpers in my games... but nothing seriously weird!

'The Beginning of the End' *is* a seriously weird two-parter. Apparently, you play the role of Fred (the multi-talented paper-boy who appeared in the previous games) once again. According to the nice blue piece of paper Zenobi supplied the instructions on, the evil Basil Hodgkins has made his way to the centre of the earth. Rather than finding Peter Cushing and a load of ham-actors there, he discovered the Machine Of Total Universal Control. This was built by the Incas to sustain sanity on the planet. Before you could say "What sanity?", Basil had dismantled the machine and scattered its parts through time and space. What you have to do, as Fred, is retrieve all the pieces.

The beginning of the game is sane enough. You are in your French class and you must escape. You can't go through the door, but doing a Michael Palin ('Pole to Pole') will at least enable you to get the window open. If you watch where you stand you'll be able to get out with a few vital objects – one of which, the clock, does far more than tell the time. After a quick chat with a workman, you take advantage of a mishap and dive, from the ledge outside the classroom, into the school's pool. No use trying to swim, but a careful examination will yield one of the components and pulling the plug will take you somewhere else entirely.

Here things start getting interesting. There are plenty of locked doors, magic potions, and objects with very strange names. For example, your job in this section is to find the Super-conductive Nucleosonic Power Transannihilator – and, believe me, that's one of the more sensible monikers! There's plenty of people to meet and chat with. The wizard will let you take some stuff if you ask nicely. The mermaid is after a tooth, the gypsy is after a nice necklace, while the poor old gardener just wants to be left alone.

The game is very tricky and it takes a lot of work to get through the first part. You shouldn't trust the author too much – don't think that every lever or button you come across should have to be pulled or pushed; sometimes this has undesirable effects.

Part two starts off in a barn and your first job is to get hold of an egg. Maybe you can get the nearby hen to offer some assistance?

The humour is quirky and not too overstated – not amazingly funny, but enough to bring a few grins to your face. I think that a little bit of humour helps liven a game up, even a serious one.

You'll probably find yourself going around in circles a lot (sometimes it won't be your fault as some of the answers are only obvious once you know the solution) but it's worth persevering with through to the end.

To sum it up: A challenging game that I recommend, but only to those adventurers with a few games under their belt already.

```
******The Beginning of the End******
Part of the pirates' lair, this
lost treasure chamber's walls
are painted gold — probably
fool's gold! There is a
prestigious treasure chest here,
though.

Exit(s): W.
»EXAMINE CHEST
On it is no lock, and many
jewels are glued to it — they're
obviously paste! I notice a
small hole in its side, in which
a cork is stuffed.
»I
I have with me: an airtight
container and an aristocratic
corkscrew.
»«
```

Having co-authored two fractal graphics type-ins that were featured in Your Sinclair magazine, Jonathan Scott spent a large chunk of the 1990s writing adventures for Zenobi Software. Teaming up with his regular collaborator Stephen Boyd on many of them, the games produced were often humorous and always pretty unique.

The Black Knight (Spectrum 48K)

Written by Mandy Rodrigues

Published by Atlas Adventure Software / The Guild

```
habitation to the west bathed
in the warm sunlight.To the
north,beyond a wide river,the
valley is shrouded in haze.A
path leads north.
> n
You stand at a crossroads where
winding paths lead north,south,
east and west.The valley,green
and fragrant,lies all around
you.Birds chirp as they fly
through the blue sky,riding on
a gentle warm breeze.
> n
You are on a narrow north south
path bordered to the east and
west by thick undergrowth.From
the north you can hear the
faint sound of lapping water.You
 also notice an ugly little
dwarf
> examine dwarf
An ugly little fellow.
>
```

'Black Knight' is an old GACed game that hails from about 1988. It was written by Mandy Rodrigues, a former editor of the 'Adventure Probe' fanzine, and now 'Bash The Barbarian' of Commodore Force. She originally published the game on her Atlas Adventure Software label, but when she had to stop producing 'Probe' (and was succeeded by Barbara Gibb) she passed on the Spectrum games in her catalogue (this game and 'The Case Of The Mixed Up Shymer' by Sandra Sharkey) over to Tony Collins of The Guild.

'Black Knight' doesn't come with any documentation, just the standard The Guild cassette box, and as there's no in-game intro you may be at a bit of a loss not knowing who you are and what you're out to do in the game. Having finished the adventure I'll tell you that you're Sir Galahad and your task is to slay the Black Knight of the game's title.

The adventure comes in two GACed parts, the second accessed by a password. In both bits the screen presentation is very poor, but that is typical with many GACed games, however the screen colours are cyan paper and black text which are quite easy on the eyes.

Part one starts at the entrance to a beautiful valley. Quite atmospheric text describes this first, and all subsequent, locations. The puzzles range from very easy to average in this adventure, making the game good for beginners. Unusually for a GAC adventure the command SEARCH is useful on more than one occasion.

In this first part you'll find yourself carrying out tasks as diverse as milking a cow and defeating an evil force (in the cave near the end of this part). There are a few characters around, like the drunken warlock and the dwarf but most of it hinges around objects among which are interesting items like a lodestone, some mistletoe and a chastity belt!

Once over a bridge and having done a bit of a William Tell, you'll be ready to load up the second part of the game. This part seemed to me to be a lot shorter and a lot easier with only the inclusion of a maze to make it appear a bit bigger.

There's not really much to do before you meet and defeat the Knight. Only the leopard and the noisy soldiers (whom Mandy seems reluctant to kill off) will really give you any problems.

```
Before you lies a dark forest.A
great menhir stands as if
guarding the northeast and
northwest paths into the
forbidding interior.The wind
moans through the trees as if
warning you to turn back.You
also notice a length of twisted
hemp
>get hemp
You get a length of twisted
hemp
>ne
You are in a small clearing to
the east of the Menhir.The
trail bends northwest and
southwest.To the south a small
hovel nestles between the trees.
You also notice a broken pot
>get pot
You get a broken pot
>examine pot
Useless.
>
```

So, although the game isn't that big or difficult it is quite enjoyable and atmospheric (there's lots of flashes of lightning and mysterious voices around). A nice game to load up if you're getting stuck in another title to give your mind a break and boost your confidence a bit. Maybe it's a tad overpriced, £2 would have been a better mark, but you do get two chunks of adventure for your money.

The Black Tower (Spectrum 48K)

Written by Diane Rice

Published by Zenobi Software

'The Black Tower' (why is it that there are always black or white towers? Why not green ones, or pink with blue spots?) is a Quilled game that spans two parts and sets you on the task of retrieving yet another crystal (this one's the Morjan Crystal) from the Black Tower. Unusually though, you have to destroy it once you've found it.

The first half of the game reminds me of some of Laurence Creighton's adventures. The Quill adventure writing utility only has a limited number of flags, nowhere near enough to keep track of everything that happens in a more complicated game. To construct a longer experience you need to put in various one-way routes where the player cannot retrace his or her steps. That way, you can re-use the flags, that you've previous used, for other things. 'The Black Tower' has several of these 'points of no return'.

```
You are in a hut.
It does not appear to be lived
in at the moment as the sandy
floor is clean and tidy and
the central hearth is cold.
****************************************
I'm ready for your instructions
>EXAMINE HEARTH

A circle of large stones built
to contain a fire.

I'm ready for your instructions
>EXAMINE FLOOR

Sandy and smooth.

I await your command.
>
```

The puzzles in the earlier part of the adventure are quite straightforward and are arranged thoughtfully so that players don't get stuck too stuck early on. There's a delightful gnome character who raised a chuckle from me on several occasions. The creatures and locations in this game are definitely unusual and it all helps give the adventure have a different flavour than the millions of other 'get an object from the castle/tower' games that I've played in the past.

At the end of the first part you are given a password so that you can enter part two. Your password depends on which objects you're carrying at the end of the first part, though you will get a gentle hint later on if you've picked the wrong one.

The puzzles get even trickier in the second part. Don't be afraid of restarting this section of the adventure to check if you've missed something. Despite the spike in difficulty it's well worth battling through right to the end of the tale.

Overall, this is a great first adventure from a new author. I'm not going to tell you any more about the game as it would spoil your enjoyment of it.... mind you, what would spoil your enjoyment more would be if you didn't buy it. Don't make that mistake!

Celtic Carnage (Spectrum 48K)

Written by The Traveller in Black (Ian S. Brown)

Published by Zenobi Software

His life-force faded... his vision dimmed and Phoenix was reborn again. This time Phoenix had been sent to the land of Erin, the home of a great race of warriors known as the Celts.

Once again the need is great... the Celts are on the verge of defeat. Medb, the queen of Connacht has crossed the border on a raid that, though initially to steal only the prize bull, will slaughter the Celts and conquer Ulster. The Celts are in no shape to stop her for they have been laid low by the terrible sickness known as Cess Noinden Ulad and are further hindered by the fact that Medb has called upon the forces of the Primal Darkness to help... a whole legion of demons are at her command.

Phoenix started the adventure on Cromm's Crest before the fortress known as Emain Macha. Inside were some of the Celts and King Conchobar Mac Nessa. It was there that Phoenix learned of his quest... he must seek out Cathbad the High Druid, the only person who can cure the disease, and also the man known as Cuchulainn, the hero of Ulster who has disappeared in mysterious circumstances.

And so, Phoenix started out on his task. He was not without help. Most people would give him some information when he TALKed to them. The majority of them told him to seek out someone... yet when he found that someone they told him to go and see someone else. One such person he needed to find was Sualtaim, the foster father of Cuchlainn. He wasn't very far away... or at least his head wasn't, it occupied an upturned shield on a table in the kitchens of the fort and miraculously still lived. He said that Phoenix's best bet was to find Loeg, one of Cuchulainn's closest friends.

Phoenix had plenty of other people to seek out first. The High Druid refused to help cure the sickness until he found out what fate had befallen his foster son. Phoenix found a child about the right age impaled on an idol of Clochar, but the demon Cermand Cestach that commanded the statue refused to let the body free.

Phoenix came across the sacred bull quite early but gave its keeper a nasty shock. Beyond the bull there were several dangers, but all of these were overcome with a bit of crafty combat using objects found nearby and also found early on in the adventure, after a lot of SEARCHing and EXAMining.

```
This western corner is where the
warriors' horses are normally
kept tethered. Only two horses
remain and these have had their
throats ripped out. You may go
to the north-east or south-east.
[O I O]  [O I O]  [O I O]  [O I O]
What now, Phoenix?

I
You have with you
a pair of LEATHER BOOTS (worn)
a BLACK ROBE (worn)

What should you do now?
```

Elsewhere Phoenix encountered an aged hag that was not all she appeared to be and who helped him contact Loeg, once he had satisfied her riddle. Loeg was anxious to join his friend and he proved invaluable in helping Phoenix get from place to place. Demons seemed to be everywhere but Phoenix was normally given adequate warning of them.

Some of the demons Phoenix encountered were in human form. He journeyed far and wide to the very depths of the Otherworld to contact the gods. He learned about the Celtic culture and their legends and needed to remember all he was told carefully for it was bound to be of great use later on.

After rescuing Culchulainn and defeating the evil Gore, Loeg and Phoenix joined the hero of Ulster in the final battle. It took skill, bravery and a few objects picked up on the way but eventually the forces of Chronos triumphed. But the evil Primal Darkness would undoubtedly return and again Phoenix would be reborn. He hoped so... he had enjoyed this adventure.

('Celtic Carnage' is another excellent game by the Traveller. The myths and culture of the Celts has been cleverly crafted into a brilliant adventure that I thoroughly enjoyed battling through right to the end. It was, perhaps, a little easier than the previous three Phoenix games but there was definitely a lot to do and I had an enthralling time playing through the game.

Negative points? Well, the screen layout was a bit untidy, sometimes with extra blank lines between the location description and the scroll-bar, and the parser was occasionally a little unfriendly and failed to accept what I thought were perfectly valid synonyms. All of this can easily be ignored as the game is probably the best of the series so far.

Conman the Barbaric (Spectrum 48K)

Written by Jason Nicholls

Published by The Elven Adventurers / Northern Underground

    'Conman the Barbaric' starts quite promisingly, with a nice title screen that dissolves away to reveal the starting location.

    The first thing you notice is the interesting screen layout, with images and information displayed at the top and scrolling text underneath.

    There are various status indicators dotted around and the exits from each location are depicted through a series of icons. There's also a picture of a face on one side of the screen. This is either of a character who is in the same location as you or a picture of yourself. These portraits are excellently done and are accompanied by a simplistic but effective graphic of the location.

Of course, all these pictures eat up a large chunk of memory and that means there is less room for everything else. The text is certainly very short, there are not too many locations and there are hardly any objects to interact with or puzzles to solve.

There's no scene-setting introduction, either, so I had no clue what my actual quest was. You begin in a village where, judging from the sparse location description, you used to live and work as a blacksmith. Presumably I was Conman, the titular hero, who had designs on becoming a fearless barbarian?

Dotted around you are an estate agents, a weapon shop and a pawnbrokers. There's also a wagon parked up nearby and it's very tempting to take a ride in it straight away. If you leave these initial locations too soon, though, you'll will have missed a key item that any decent barbarian needs to make his (or her!) way in the world.

When you're finally ready for the wagon ride it takes you to a new town isn't much bigger than the first, although it's padded out by the inclusion of a maze. Here, once again, I found myself wandering around quite aimlessly, still baffled as to what my ultimate objective was. Eventually I managed to make my way through a haphazard chain of events and half-puzzles and triggered the ending of the game without really feeling much sense of achievement.

The game is obviously designed as a parody of common

fantasy scenarios and throughout the adventure, juvenile and toilet humour is plentiful. It only really succeeds in being funny in a few instances. There are far too many fourth-wall breaking nods to the fact this is an adventure game and not enough actual adventure game puzzles and world building.

Conman is presented as a three-part adventure but the second and third parts can be played independently, making the password given to you at the end of part one redundant. I imagine that the three sections, individually titled 'Realm of Death', 'City of Thieves' and 'Sea of Blood', were envisaged as a trilogy. The problem is that, despite the nice variation in settings and themes across the instalments, there just isn't enough adventure or plot there for one game, let alone three.

Conman had the potential to be a great game but ultimately ends up being a pretty, but shallow one. Despite the care and attention taken on the visual side of things the game's puzzles are pretty lacklustre. I get the feeling that Jason and Co. did the graphics first and then decided to fit an adventure to them. They didn't totally succeed.

Corporal Stone (Spectrum 48K)

Written by James Taylor

Published by Zenobi Software

```
A lion.

>EXAMINE LION
The lion, who must have escaped
from the local circus, is
writhing around in agony. The
source of its discomfort is a
thorn stuck in its paw, which it
can't dislodge.

>REMOVE THORN
You remove the thorn and the
lion breathes a sigh of relief.
"Thank you kind sir. If you are
ever in a dangerous situation,
by saying my name, you will
summon me and I will help. But
you can only do this once."
"But what is your name?" you
enquire.
"Oxo." The lion bounds off into
the distance.

          PRESS A KEY
```

If somebody told me that they'd just come across aliens
from outer space, killer toys, a lion, a hyena and Lucifer himself
at their local shopping centre then I'd be very inclined to call the
men in the white coats. However, if you're a government agent
and have several dead bodies on your hands, apparently killed
by these phenomena, then you have no choice but to investigate.
And that's your task in this QUILLed tale.

You start off in the parking lot of the centre next to your
car and also next to the body of one of your colleagues, Ivan. He

mumbles something along the lines of, "They got me.... kill the little people.... squaaaa...", and then chooses that moment to die. Why, does that always happen, eh? Oh well, better explore the centre. But first you'll need to take a look inside your car (remembering what these vehicles normally contain as there's no mention of certain points of interest; it's up to you to use your brain).

From the car-park you can either take the lift up, or have a walk outside. The lift is rather eerie, as although there are five buttons in it, only the buttons marked 1 and 2 work. Pressing the other 3 merely produce the sound of distant laughter.

Taking the lift to the 2nd floor gets you to six shops. Four of these are instantly accessible and you can wander in and out of them to your heart's content without anybody even coming up to you and saying, "Can I help you?". In the gardening shop you'll encounter some very strange gnomes and a pile of manure that you'll have to get to grips with. Curiously, the shop assistant here only speak French.

The clothes shop has a stereotypical, bubble-gum blowing woman in charge who has had her knitting needles pinched. She needs them to finish the pullover she's making. I was mildly amused by the image of this girl blowing gum and knitting simultaneously.

A good bet might be to check out the book-keepers next but the most action is to be found in the toyshop. It contains a kid who takes great delight in throwing a plastic brick at you. There's also the obligatory clown in a box ("Do you want a present?", "Have a nice day!") and yet another dead body. The cause of this? Take a closer look at the train set.

Yobs block the entrance to the other two shops but you shouldn't have much problems in getting past them. In the bookshop I spotted a handy revision aid whilst in the Sports Shop there's an assistant in a shell-suit who's rather partial to Pot Noodles!

Outside the building you'll come across an almost biblical lion with a familiar name, a hyena and Lucifer (dressed in a purple suit!). You also get to play at being Fireman Sam as well as uncover the lost treasure of Bea T Max!

The game is full of unusual and crazy happenings and some funny text in places. There's quite a bit to do. You have to really work to pick up the points in this game, but I couldn't help feeling that the game could have done with a few more locations.

Presentation is good, especially for The Quill, and you can choose between two fonts. Ramsave and Ramload are included but there's no GET ALL feature.

To sum it up – a good first adventure from James Taylor. Sometimes tricky and nearly always enjoyable.

Corya – Warrior Sage (Spectrum 48K)

Written by Anthony Collins

Published by The Guild

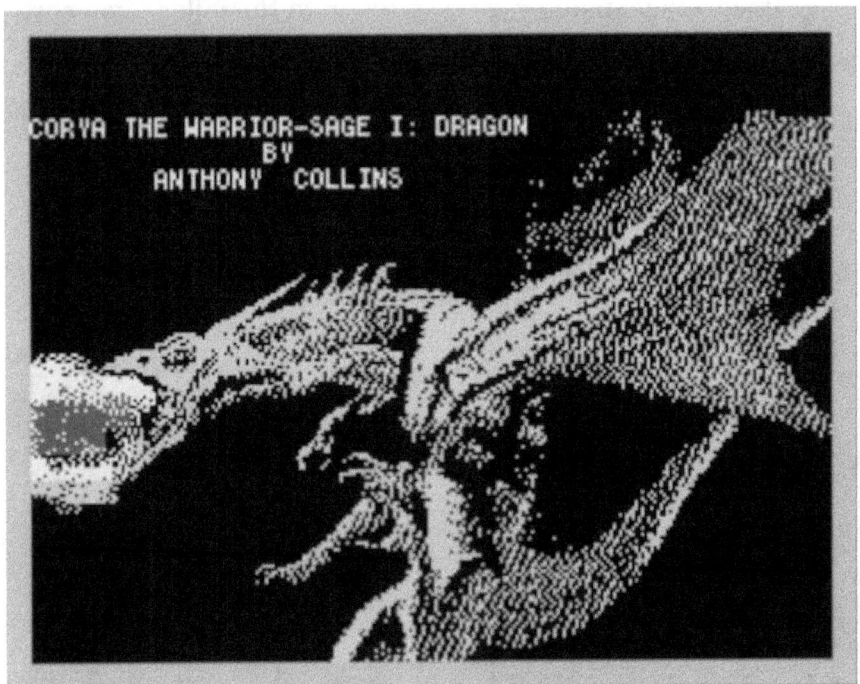

In the land of Tanna, there is a legend. A legend of a warrior sage; a mighty magician who was once a member of the Temple of Wisdom but chose to venture into the world of man. The legend tells of Corya, and how he is seldom seen unless the need is so great that only he can help. This is the story of one of those times. A time where many died, and much devastation occurred. A time when the remaining villages prayed and Corya appeared...

So starts the tale which unfolds in Tony Collins' two part

adventure 'Corya – The Warrior Sage'. You, as Corya, stand atop the hill overlooking the village. A quick INVENTORY call reveals several things: That you are clad in typical adventuring gear and that you carry a spell book.

Once you've made your way down to the village you come across the villagers. In their terrified state they are frightened to see a stranger in their midst, but peace and harmony can soon be restored with a bit of spell casting.

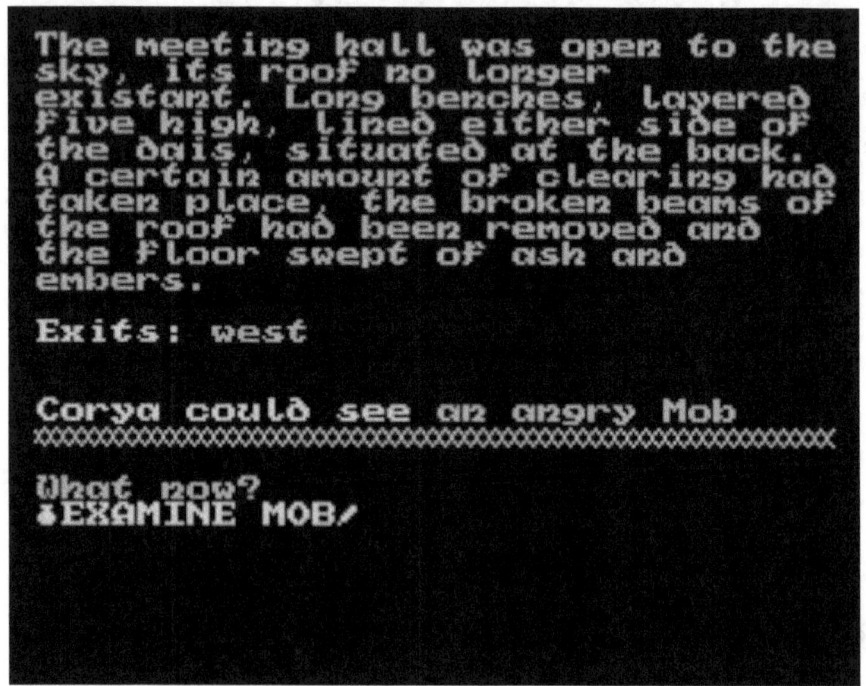

With that done, Entur, the head of the village council, asks for your help to dispose of the dragon whose lair lies in the mystical mountains of Caithen-La-Ethin. You say yes, and the villagers promise to help you in any way they can. One of your first tasks involves mending your sword. But where is the blacksmith? He hasn't been seen since the dragon's attack.

Being a warrior sage, Corya has several spells at his disposal – FIRE, HEAL, CHERISH and SHIELD. It proves vital that you take notice of their properties as you'll have to make full use of them to get past several puzzles.

The game has a carefully planned, very linear, book-like structure and the action takes place in groups of locations. These locations and their respective problems form chapters of the story which are linked by pages of text (which help to keep the action moving and maintain the atmosphere).

The atmosphere is further enhanced by the lengthy location text. It's a real treat to read and makes Tony Collins' mystical world seem totally real and believable.

Corya is an easy game to get hooked on and you'll be up against tough problems up to and beyond your conflict with the dragon at the end. If I had any gripes about the game at all it would be that it's all over a bit too soon. However, it left me really looking forward to another outing as Corya.

Overall, Corya is one adventure you must get, especially if you like your games to be of the deep, atmospheric kind. Highly recommended.

The Curse of Calutha (Spectrum 48K)

Written by Laurence Creighton

Published by Zenobi Software

```
You are on the muddy bank of a
small, deep lake.  Across the
lake to the east is a cottage;
to the north a church,and across
the lake to the northeast you
see a sandy shore.  To the south
is a dense forest.
Paths lead north, south and west

YOU CAN SEE:-
A small boat

*EXAMINE BOAT
A closer scrutiny reveals that
there is a tiny hole in the side

*I
INVENTORY:
Some loose change

**
```

I've had 'Curse of Calutha' sitting on my shelves of software for quite some time and I never seemed to get around to playing it properly. But at last, with the amazing appearance of Easter, free time materialised and the chance to play it came...

'Calutha' was written by the master of Spectrum QUILLed adventures Laurence Creighton. Unusually, for him, it's a two-part adventure.

The plot goes something like this... You've always been one for tales of lost treasure and so when you hear the story of

Calutha, while on a hiking trip, and of his great treasure which he hid in a place called the Caves of Lights, you decide to have a go at tracking it down. Of course, you don't believe one word about the curse that is meant to protect the resting place of the treasure.

The game starts in a clearing where there's a deep pit. It's too deep to climb down into, but you'll undoubtedly find something around to help you. To the east is a bus stop which has the usual advertising poster... you might have trouble obtaining it at first but think what you do when you remove wallpaper or the sticky labels off the sides of tins. Also at the bus stop there's a piece of paper... it's the solution sheet to 'Calutha' but unfortunately the ink has faded and the only bit that's readable tells you about some of the command abbreviations and not to say CALUTHA. Believe me, don't type CALUTHA... well, not unless you've saved your game first.

There are plenty of objects lying around in the first few locations. From a jam-jar to a packet of mints, they may not seem useful at first but, as this is a L.C. game, they may well be later (or they may not be!). Around the first location is a quarry, a church and a lake. The boat by the lake will probably help you cross it, but you'll need to do something about the hole in the boat's hull first.

South of the lake is a forest and (guess what?) it's a maze. It's quite easy to map and there are three locations of interest. One is by a tree which has a rope-ladder in its branches, another is a place where you'll find a tramp, while the third is the square of a small village (complete with lots of new shops and even a public house to visit).

```
You are at a bus-stop.  A notice
informs you that an industrial
dispute has ground the service
to a halt. Advertising posters
adorn the walls of the shelter.
A path leads east

YOU CAN SEE:-
A poster
A roll of mint humbugs
A sheet of paper

*GET POSTER
The poster is pasted to the wall

*GET HUMBUGS
COMMAND ACCEPTED

*GET PAPER
COMMAND ACCEPTED

**
```

The rope-ladder proves a bit of a problem at first. It's caught in a branch and the only way that you can get it free is if you climb the ladder and FREE it. The thing is, if you do that you'll then find yourself falling to the ground on the ladder (accompanied by a lovely sound FX, of which there are plenty in the game). The trick is to make sure that you stay up, while the ladder goes down... pretty simple if you really get to grips with the problem (and the tree!)

As I mentioned before, there are a lot of objects around and you'll need to ferry these about quite a bit (sometimes literally) because of the limit on the number of items that you can carry at any one time. When you do eventually get across the lake, don't think that you won't be coming back... believe me you'll be crossing that lake more than once in this game.

Part two is entered by the use of a password and is more of the same sort of thing... there's even another boat and another lake to cross. You start in the Caves of Light, although you don't really stay there for long. This part does seem to be a bit bigger than the first bit, but if anything I'd say that it was slightly easier... though maybe I found it easier because I was more in tune with the author after the first part. There's even a nice little old wizard to meet and who'll give you a bit of a hand if you've got something he wants.

Laurence's text is pretty minimal when it comes to location descriptions, probably due to the memory restrictions of the Quill utility but he still manages to incorporate a lot of hints into the text (and you'll no doubt need these!).

Overall – 'Calutha' is definitely a game full of puzzles and plenty to do. It can get a bit tedious in places when you find yourself having constantly to retrace your steps but the puzzles are interesting and original enough to keep you wanting to press on further into the game. Not one for the inexperienced adventurer but it will keep the more seasoned hands busy (and John Wilson, sending out help-sheets) for quite a while.

The Dark Tower (Spectrum 48K)

By Jack Lockerby

Published by Zenobi Software

Hot on the heels of 'The Ellisnore Diamond' is yet another game from the PAW of Jack Lockerby. Being a great River fan, I was looking forward to another solid, reliable game from Jack, but I certainly wasn't expecting this... What? – Read on and find out!

The bitter struggle between the humans and the orcs ended when the evil Dark Lord was killed. Some orcs, however, survived and it was these that took to roaming round the countryside looting and pillaging as they went. It wasn't long before they set their sights on the Monastery of Oraghag, famous for its Golden Chalice. It was this chalice that they stole and took back to their Dark Tower, which lay beyond the Shadow Mountains. To add insult to injury, they also captured the leader of the unicorn herd and subjected it to horrific tortures before releasing it back into the forest.

Your task is simple. You must recover the stolen items from the orcs and befriend the unicorn, as it is your only possible method of transport back to the monastery.

The game starts in the forest. To the north you can see a wisp of smoke. What could it be? By venturing closer you find out that it's a house, but the owner won't let you in. Maybe the smoke gives a clue to the answer to this first, and excellent, problem.

Elsewhere you come across a tall tree and up that is a bird. There's a valuable object in the nest, but how are you meant to get it when the bird is watching over you? Then there's an unmarked grave, and a pool which needs to be noted. And where has that orc, which you came across in the forest, run off to? Should you expect orc reinforcements soon?

All the above are standard adventuring fare, but there's plenty that's original, fresh and bloody baffling! Take the portal that you find in the forest, for instance. When you try to go through it, a mysterious force drives you back. So how do you go through? Well, the answer lies in the runes engraved on it. Mind you, it's not that simple because you can't read the runes at first!

Two real gems of an object come in the form of a ring and

a black sack. The ring has several powers that you need to find out about, not least the old Bilbo Baggins type one. Then there is the bottomless sack which has more uses than just putting objects in it, I can tell you.

Of course, all these complex objects do take their toll on the old programming. The ring behaved a bit strangely on me a couple of times, but then that's magical objects for you, right? Very unpredictable.

```
EAST BRANCH
   YOU ARE NEAR THE END OF A
STOUT, SNOW-COVERED BRANCH, THAT
HANGS OUT OVER THE FOREST TRAIL,
FAR BELOW.
   YOU CAN SEE A LARGE BIRD
GUARDING HER NEST.
..................................................
   EXITS: W,
..................................................
EXAMINE BIRD
   IT'S QUITE BIG!
EXAMINE NEST
   IT CONTAINS A PAIR OF DICE.
GET DICE
   THE BIRD FLIES UP AND DRIVES
YOU BACK!
■
```

The first puzzles are a right mixture, with some easy and some hard, but that's how it should be. At points the game will have you tearing your hair out and you'll reset, but you'll always be reloading it again for 'just one more go!' – A sign of a good game. Before long you'll meet the unicorn, but he seems rather scared of you! Another problem lies in a huge orc with a large axe – Time for the ramsave, methinks!

Talking about the games features. They include the usual RAMSAVE (RS), RAMLOAD (RL), QUIT(Q), SCORE(SC), GET ALL and DROP ALL etc. The screen layout is very well designed, with Jack's usual instant screen update method, and a very good font, though slightly boring, that appears in two sizes to highlight certain things in the text.

The game is full of things to do, and is very well presented, designed, written, and programmed. A lot of people are calling this Jack's best game to date, and I can only agree. This is one you really must get!

Deathbringer (Spectrum 48K)

Written by Trevor Whitsey

Published by The Guild

. . Slowing its approach, the Orbital entered the Solar System, undetected by the SCAN network.
As Retro-jets ignited, the Reptillians departed, tracked only by a fine trail of vapour. Intent only on their objective, they descended rapidly through the atmosphere of the blue, mist-covered planet below. Little did they know the fate that awaited, for their Death Search had begun . .

In Trevor Whitsey's sci-fi tale 'Deathbringer' you play the part of a young space cadet. Your mission is to find the ultimate weapon named Deathbringer before it falls into the hands of the evil Reptillians.

Your quest starts in a hut in the Amazon and by exploring your immediate surroundings you find a room with a huge viewscreen in it. Also here is your companion for the adventure, a mechanised flying thing called the Globe.

Once you've collected the equipment left for you, your

first task is to make your way to the alien flying saucer that is up on top of a steep hill; one too difficult to climb by foot. Luckily the Globe helps out here and you're soon up to and into the spaceship.

The first difficulty is flying the darn thing – All the controls are in alien and hitting them 'willy nilly' is definitely not a good idea with a Reptillian battle-cruiser in hot pursuit.

'Deathbringer' is a PAWed adventure but the text scrolls continuously upwards, rather than under the location text fixed in place at the top. There are a few spelling and grammar mistakes, but otherwise the text is moderately atmospheric and quite convincing. (I did find it a bit strange that you could remove your uniform even when you had the spacesuit on over it!)

Overall, Deathbringer is an okay sci-fi game that lacks the sparkle and polish of similar titles like 'Captain Kook' and 'Magnetic Moon', but it will probably keep any sci-fi addict happy for an evening or two.

Diarmid (Spectrum 48K)

By Dennis Francombe

Published by Zenobi Software

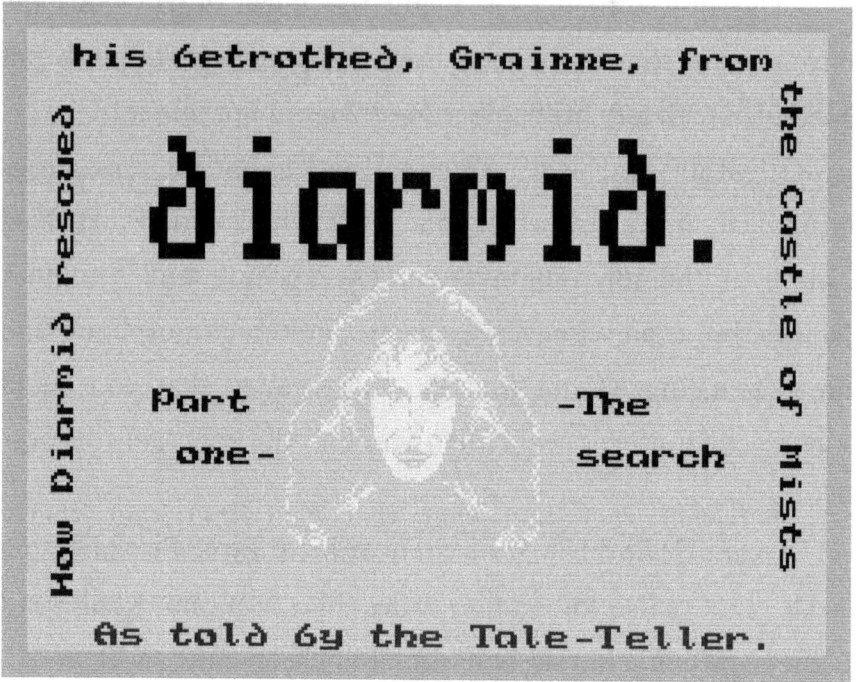

As 'Diarmid', the Fenian Hero, you were to be betrothed to the fair and lithesome Grainne. Unfortunately, the evil Black MacMorna has captured her and imprisoned her in the Castle of The Mists. It's up to you to rescue her.

You will find yourself journeying across the Lost Lands taking in the wondrous sights (all described nicely by Dennis) and meeting all manner of creatures. Dennis seems to prefer encounters with animals in his games than with people, though beware, for not all animals are as they appear.

Later on you take to the high seas where it is a good idea to be a bit of a Horatio Hornblower and come dashing to the rescue. There are a lot of tricky puzzles between here and the citadel of Black MacMorna and many of them have a magical solution. The atmosphere is brilliant and great care seems to have been taken in producing a believable world to roam in.

Part two sees you teaming up with Bran, a large dog that will perform certain tasks for you. Controlled in the usual way (Say to Bran "xxx") Bran will be helpful on more than one occasion. Part two requires the password you obtained at the end of the first bit (thankfully there's no horrible saving of tape data needed). This section is more of a traditional exploration adventure although there are enough twists and turns to keep you busy if you're serious about rescuing Grainne.

The presentation is quite good with a nice use of text colours, but I still think the screen layout could have been a bit tidier.

I didn't really like Dennis's 'Fisher King' but I really liked 'Diarmid' and recommend it worth buying if you too like descriptive, atmospheric, almost period adventures.

Dragon Slayer (Spectrum 48K & 128K)

Written by Martin Freemantle

Published by Dreamworld Adventures

Martin Freemantle, a familiar name to 'Adventure Probe' readers (and those who go to the London Adventure get-togethers) has launched a new Spectrum adventure label called 'Dreamworld Adventures'. His first release is 'Dragon Slayer' and it looks quite impressive.

'Dragon Slayer' comes in two versions. The first is a 128K one-part while the second is a 48K two-parter. According to Martin, the 48K version is actually better because it was done second and he had learnt a lot since programming the first part (his first adventure). In the 48K version you need to load a saved position into part two in order to continue playing.

The setting is a typical fantasy one, with a nice great big war going on between the goblins (the bad guys) and the humans (the good guys... mainly on account of you being a human. Why can't we play the bad guys in adventures for a change?). The plot revolves around a magical medallion called the 'Circle of Nine' that gives the wearer protection against anything. This medallion was made by a human warlock but has unfortunately been nabbed by the evil Goblins (and who knows what purpose they will put it to!) Basically, what you have to do is kill the silver dragon, who's formed an alliance with the Goblins.

On loading you're treated to some adequate graphics and information about the various game commands. Most are standard adventuring fare... STORY gives you background info, INFO lists what I'm basically typing out now, VOCAB shows some words that you can use, and START shows the first few locations that you should have on your map.

Your initial progress is hindered by a huge horrible Goblin that won't let you across a bridge. Not exactly a new puzzle but one that will have you scratching your head for a little while. In these first locations it pays to EXAMINE and SEARCH everything and also to read the location text very carefully.

The room descriptions are short and to the point. Below the text are 'Compass Software' style compass points and two rather hefty swords. The 128K version features a lot of animation. For example, at one point you encounter a worm and you see it wriggle across the screen and disappear.

The parser is a bit unfriendly and there is a tendency for obscure inputs when quite simple ones would suffice.

Overall, a good first attempt at producing an adventure by Martin. It's obvious that he's learnt a lot from the process so I look forward to seeing his next adventure (the second part of this tale).

Martin Freemantle's 'Dragon Slayer' ended up being the first game of a trilogy released on the Spectrum; joined later by 'Death or Glory' and 'The Final Battle'. Dreamworld Adventures released over a dozen adventures during the early 1990s including titles by another frequent 'Adventure Probe' contributor and playtester, Sharon Harwood.

Dreamare (Spectrum 48K)

Written by Jason Nicholls

Published by The Elven Adventures / Northern Underground

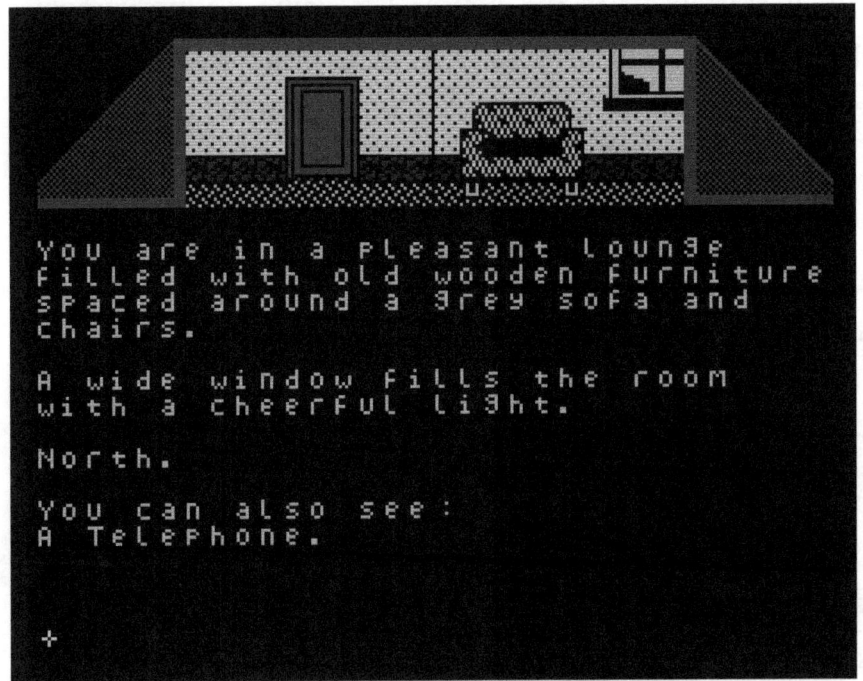

After playing 'The Haunting' earlier on in the day I wasn't really looking forward to slogging through another Elven Adventurers game... especially as this one seemed to suffer from the same presentation faults. But after a few minutes at the keyboard I realised that this game was something a little bit different.

The game came in the standard 'Northern Underground' box with no documentation whatsoever, but from piecing together information from various N.U. adverts I found out that the basic idea of the game is to somehow save your little sister from the evil demon that is terrorising her dreams and will eventually kill her.

The game is a two-parter and in the first section ('The Day') I started off in my house. The game features graphics which are very well done. In this first part they are split into two little sections. For example, one section has a wall with a door in it, the other section may have the wall with a drawer against it or a car or something. These are 'glued' together on screen to build up different pictures of the various places you come across with the minimum amount of hassle. You can turn them off by PIX OFF but I found that they livened up the presentation when left on.

Checking my inventory, I found that I had 250 dollars and 'not a sausage'... by the currency I surmised that the adventure was set in the good old U.S. of A. After a brief exploration of the house I found a few items and also the locked door of my sister's bedroom (presumably she is inside asleep!). Parked outside the house was my red 'Cabillac' (which spookily changed into a Cadillac when I entered it... a spelling mistake methinks!) which started at the mere press of a button. All I had to do was type DRIVE TO somewhere and I'd get there. The only thing I'd found so far was a library ticket so I thought maybe I'd best start there. Sure enough, DRIVE TO LIBRARY got me to the appropriate destination and once inside I was informed by the nice librarian that my magazine had arrived. Magazine? What magazine?

It turned out that it was a magazine about the supernatural. I opened it up and found an interesting article that read as follows, grammar and spelling intact...

"All through the ages there have been reports of people being mutilated in their sleep. Many of the victims before they died confided to friends and family about a Dream Man who tortured them with horrific scenes of death and carnage. They have many names for him, Bogeyman, Lucifer, Diablo, Old Nick and the Devil amongst others. A tragic case was one of Catherine Johnston who died because of hundreds of rat bites while in her sleep. There were no explanations. Nobody knows what it is or from whence it came but there is one fact, it is deadly real."

Hmmm... The article also contained an address of the 'Dream Research Institute' where one Dr. Carol Long would be interested in hearing details of any other such cases. This seemed like the best place to proceed and after a short car journey later I found myself at the Institute. Unfortunately, Carol wasn't there but her secretary game me a number that I could contact.

And after that... well, wait a minute I'm giving too much away. Let's just say that it involved more travelling and piecing together clues. The way this first part works is that you drive to one place and get information which will tell you where to head to and what to look up next. Eventually, you'll get in touch with the family of Catherine Johnston and gain access to her diary. You'll decide that the only way to free your sister is to fight with this Devil yourself, and so you follow in the footsteps of Catherine and gather the equipment needed to send you into the deep sleep needed for the Dreamare.

Once you've achieved the dream state part one ends and you are given a password to the second bit. I finished part one with 115% so presumably there's some sort of scoring bug there (though I only scored for everything once!)

The second part starts with the reminder that "You are in your dreams and anything can and might happen". Indeed, that seems to be the case as I soon found myself being catapulted from situation to situation. There's a maze, it isn't too difficult, but one thing is for sure this part is much tougher than the first.

Part one is good fun and, unfriendly parser aside, is very good for beginners. It reminds me very much of Tony Collins' Methyhel which had the same sort of approach to it. Part two is difficult and you should remember that you shouldn't always do what you're told by some of the characters you meet.

Overall, I enjoyed 'Dreamare' quite a lot. It made a refreshing change to play a game that I could manage to finish the first part of quite quickly... most games these days seem to be tough from the start (or maybe I'm just getting old!). Worth checking out.

The Dungeon of Torgar (Spectrum 48K)

Written by Simon M. Langan

Published by The Guild

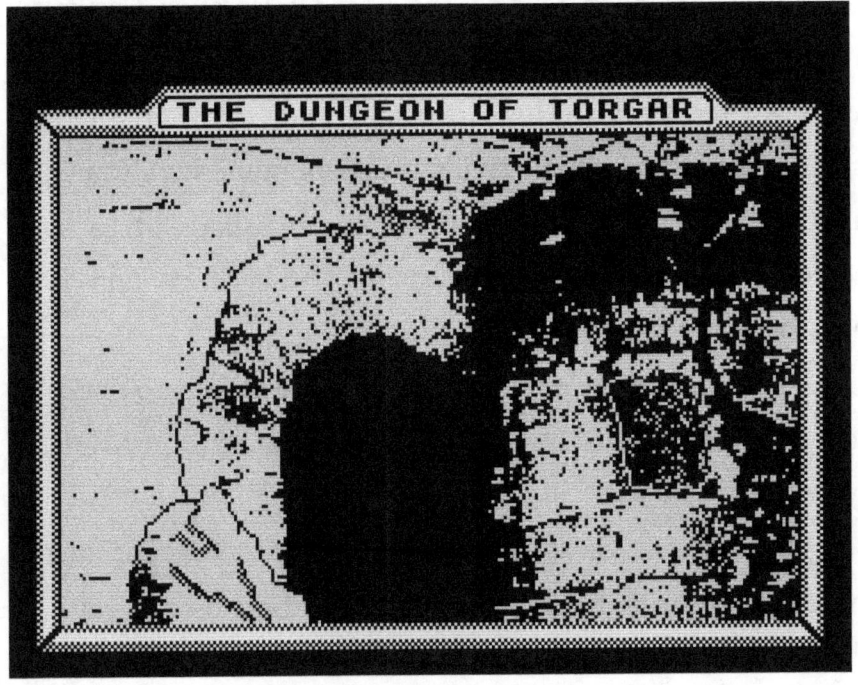

The 'Dungeon of Torgar' contains a legendary hoard of treasure and you've decided to go and retrieve the lot for some reason. (Guess who hasn't got the instructions!)

You start outside the entrance to the fabled dungeon. Lying beside you is a lamp, which it's a good idea to pick up and light. When you enter the dungeon, a portcullis closes behind you and you're told that there's "No way out!"

Once inside you find that there's some sort of temple, filled with worshippers to the god Torgar. Making sure that you keep out of the way of them should be your first priority, then after a bit of 'idol'ness you should find yourself in the dungeon proper.

Glancing at the piece of parchment that you are carrying, shows that you need to find the Cup Of Dreams, Crown Of Kings, Jade Statue, Cloak Of Gold, Shield Of Protection, Demon's Eye, Book Of The Universe, Wand Of Power, Sun Star and the Vase Of The Sky. That's some shopping list! Your task will be anything but easy as there are guardians of all sorts protecting the treasure; from snakes to skeletons and from death-beasts to rock-beasts.

There are also plenty of none-treasure objects to find. The most dangerous has to be the 'Eye of Medusa'. If you EXAMINE it you'll turn to stone!

It's not just the objects that you have to watch out for. There's a leprechaun who will both help and hinder you. He takes a liking to a little silver flute you've found. In fact if you give it to him he'll play Irish jigs on it. He also whispers rude jokes, adjusts his hat, feels in his pocket and has the annoying habit of clicking his fingers and making your lamp go out.

Overall, 'Torgar' is quite a challenging game from The Guild. It has several text layout problems and suffers from the standard Guild conversion presentation problem of every game looking the same.

The Ellisnore Diamond (Spectrum 48K)

Written by Jack Lockerby

Published by Zenobi Software

```
CHANDLER'S SHOP
  YOU ARE STANDING AT THE COUNTER
AND ON THE OTHER SIDE IS AN OLD
MAN. ON THE COUNTER ARE SOME
TINDER-BOXES AND KNIVES.
.........................................
 EXITS: OUT.
.........................................
  THE OLD MAN LOOKS UP AS YOU
ENTER AND SAYS, "SOLD OUT OF
CANDLES, BUT YOU CAN BUY A KNIFE
AND A TINDER BOX."
I
YOU ARE CARRYING NOTHING.

YOU ARE WEARING YOUR USUAL
CLOTHING.
EXAMINE MAN
  HE'S JUST AN OLD MAN!
■
```

The 'Ellisnore Diamond' has an interesting history. During the English Civil War, the diamond was given to Sir Roger Durwood by King Charles the first to reward him for hiding the king in Carisbrooke Castle. But Roger betrayed the King to the roundheads and he was removed from the governorship of the castle.

Blackbeard, for that was what Sir Roger was also called (due to his black beard, no doubt!), returned to his home village of Moonholm and there he lived in isolation till he died. But

Blackbeard could not rest, even in death. His ghost walked the night, trying to find the diamond, for he had vowed that he would sell the diamond and spend the proceeds on the poor of the parish.

Where do you come in? You are a young lad who has taken upon himself the task of finding the diamond and thus help release Blackbeard's spirit from eternal damnation.

Your timing could have been better for, soon after you decide to start your quest, a severe storm devastates the village. Once the storm subsides you get under way again, well you will after you get a few things from your house. Wait a minute! Where's your front door key?

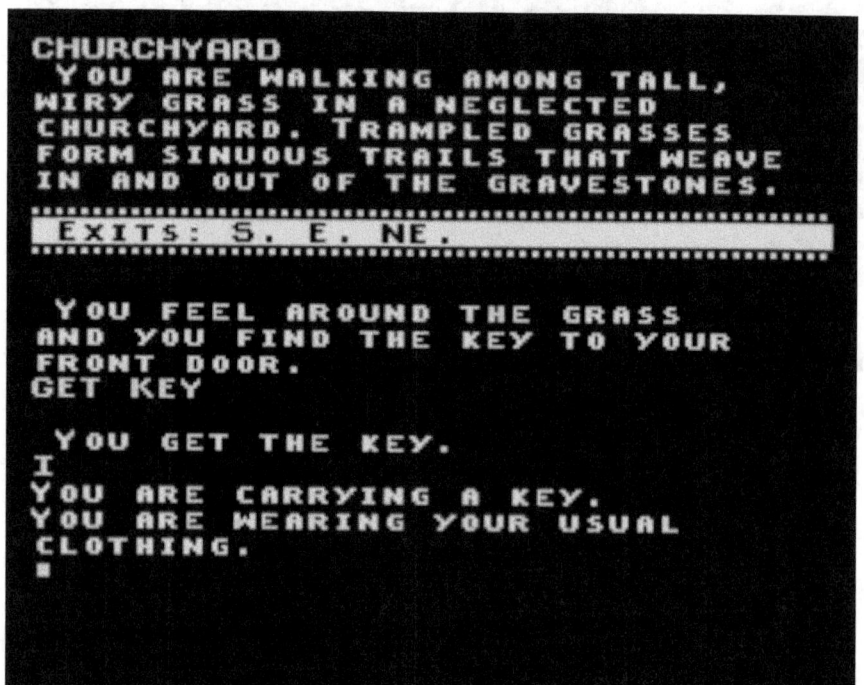

```
CHURCHYARD
  YOU ARE WALKING AMONG TALL,
WIRY GRASS IN A NEGLECTED
CHURCHYARD. TRAMPLED GRASSES
FORM SINUOUS TRAILS THAT WEAVE
IN AND OUT OF THE GRAVESTONES.
::::::::::::::::::::::::::::::::::::::::::::::
  EXITS: S. E. NE.
::::::::::::::::::::::::::::::::::::::::::::::

  YOU FEEL AROUND THE GRASS
AND YOU FIND THE KEY TO YOUR
FRONT DOOR.
GET KEY

  YOU GET THE KEY.
I
YOU ARE CARRYING A KEY.
YOU ARE WEARING YOUR USUAL
CLOTHING.
■
```

The key is to be found in another of Jack Lockerby's mazes (which is a thankfully easier one than those in 'Treasure Island'). But there are more places to visit than just the maze and you'll find that many locations contain nested puzzles. For example, you can't traverse the highway without an escort and the man who you need is in the Inn (which you can't enter due to your age!). A slippery hill proves impossible to climb, at least not without some form of suitable footwear. You could also do with the bible that the parson has, but he legs off with it as soon as you spot him!

The game is nicely put together with River's usual 'instant update' screen method. All the regular commands are here plus one or two others like the useful AGAIN command (which repeats the last action you typed).

From a technical standpoint the game isn't all that different from any of the other River titles, but it's with Jack Lockerby's writing skill that the game really comes into its own. Jack has devised his usual devious puzzles – though there's plenty there for the beginner as well. With a good plot and text to back up the puzzles, there's really no way I can fault it.

Overall, Yet another good solid game from Jack and Roger. Keep 'em coming, guys.

The Energem Enigma (Spectrum 48K)

Written by the Eighteam

Published by Precision Games / GI Games / Zenobi Software

```
YOU ARE WALKING DOWN A NARROW
  PATHWAY.  IN THE MUD ARE SOME
STRANGE TRACKS, PRESUMABLY FROM
THE PLANET'S ANIMAL LIFE. EXITS
LEAD NORTH AND SOUTH.

  ▫ ▢▢ ▫ ▢▢ ▫ ▢▢ ▫ ▢▢ ▫ ▢▢ ▫ ▢▢ ▫ ▢▢ ▫

>EXAMINE TRACKS

YOU CAN SEE A SMALL KEY THAT HAS
BEEN TRODDEN INTO THE MUD BY AN
ANIMAL.

>GET KEY
DONE

>EXAMINE KEY

A SMALL KEY.

>
```

The 'Energem Engima', for those of you who can't
remember far back into the mists of time (well, 1987 anyway!)
when the game was originally released, is the follow-up to 'The
Extricator', which is also available on the GI Games label. The
game was written with The Quill, which still seems to be an
'acceptable' utility today unlike the less popular (but still used to
good effect by certain authors) GAC. 'Energem' is a good
example of the type of games adventure writers used to produce
before they became far too clever for their own good.

The plot is this... you've just rescued old Professor Roberts from the planet ARG in the first game and you think that's the end of it. But no... Roberts, not content with you saving his life, only wants you to go and fine some Energems (rare energy-emitting gems) on an alien planet in the Glenbo system. To top it all off, the last agent sent on the mission has mysteriously disappeared and the enemy is also believed to know what you're up to. As you can see, things don't look too good, but you go anyway – well, what adventurer wouldn't, eh?

To me, the planet Edam, on which the adventure is set, seems more earth-like than alien. You'll come across several familiar objects like a well, a chest and a mattress – objects which aren't described in the (very short) location text, but only shown in the graphics. There's a few problems with that. For starters, if you turn the graphics off you'll miss these vital objects and even with them on you have to guess what the graphics are meant to portray. This is not an easy thing to do in the case of the mattress, which looks like a featureless blob!

The problems in the adventure range in difficulty, as puzzles in a good game should. Several old chestnuts appear, for example, the bucket in the well, the un-crossable rivers and ravines, the hole in the in the tree, and the hidden passage behind the waterfall. But the old puzzles are often the best, which is quite true in this case, and your search for the Energems will be anything BUT easy.

To begin with, you'll need to find all of the equipment required for the task. It's scattered in all manner of places on the planet's surface. A detector would come in handy, as would some sort of way of actually seeing the darn Energem things.

One particularly nice feature of the game is the HELP command. Type it, followed by the name of an object and you might be rewarded with a hint about its use. Believe me... you'll need all the hints you can get, especially if you're a beginner to adventuring.

Overall, the lack of good text is more than made up for by the inclusion of several devious problems and you can look on the graphics as an added bonus. Many of the earlier Quilled games have aged, but this one still looks good even after four years. Sure, it's not up to present standards and may be slightly too hard for a beginner, but at £1.99 it's well worth buying. So get it and sample the good old days once again, or maybe for the first time.

The Escaping Habit (Spectrum 48K)

By Jack Lockerby

Published by Zenobi Software

```
FENCE                    7:17 SUNDAY
You are walking alongside a high
wire fence that surrounds the
camp.
Prisoners from hut 1 are playing
football.
::::::::::::::::::::::::::::::::::::::::
Exits: N,S,W.
::::::::::::::::::::::::::::::::::::::::
Made of closely-linked steel
wire and topped with a coil of
barbed-wire. It's about 10 feet
high.
CLIMB FENCE
Several guards drag you down and
haul you off to the cooler.
Your escape plan has failed!
You have scored 0% in this
adventure and you have taken 6
turns.
          Another go?
■
```

The date is January 1942 and the place is Italy, or to be more precise, a P.O.W. camp in Italy. You are an Allied officer who was captured whilst on the way to deliver some important papers to Allied commanders in North Africa. When you were captured you were able to prevent the papers falling into enemy hands, but you have been bundled off to a small, but escape-proof, holding camp while the army contacts Berlin for further instructions on what to do with you.

You are given the 'low-down' on the camp by the senior

British officer when you arrive and told of roll-calls and the times of your meals. It is unlikely that you will ever get to eat your evening meal as the Gestapo are on their way to the camp with the intention of forcing you to reveal the hiding place of the papers, or to kill you in the process.

As it isn't such a good idea to wait around for the Gestapo you decide that the only course of action is to escape from this camp... but you'll need to do it quickly, they're coming for you at 4pm.

You start outside your hut in the camp. It's one of many such huts and, as your fellow 'room-mates' aren't here you can enter the hut and have a look round. The screen is laid out in typical Jack Lockerby style... it's neat and it automatically updates itself. I like it. The font, as usual, is readable and the exits are nice and clear.

The camp is very easy to map... though you'll need to make a separate map for each of the buildings. There are plenty of these... guards' quarters, the hospital, a library, the wash house and the cook-house. There's also a few more unusual ones, including a small church that's run by a local monk. The monk is most useful and suggests to you a plan of action... impersonate him and escape that way.

The materials that you'll need for this task will take a lot of getting. It's hard to carry things around the camp as if you're spotted carrying something unusual you'll be arrested by the guards. Small things can be hidden in your uniform pockets but for large objects you'll have to plan your route from place to place to minimise the chance of coming across a guard.

One of the most useful buildings is the theatre... access can be gained to this quite easily and I used it as a place to store all my objects. An abandoned escape route nearby may prove useful, but not for the reason that it was originally intended.

It's a very logical game but it can sometimes require very precise inputs. However, it's nowhere near as difficult as Jack's previous adventures and is a good game for the more inexperienced adventurers... I finished it in a few hours so most of you shouldn't have too many problems with it.

I could go into it in a bit more depth but then I'd give too much away about the excellent puzzles. All I can say is that it's worth buying and you should check it out as soon as possible.

The Fabled Treasure of Koosar (Spectrum 48K)

By Doreen Bardon and Arthur Simmons

Published by The Guild

```
   The beach stretches to the east
whilst to the west is a pier.
You now stand on the pebbles,
which crunch underfoot.

Also visible is...
a worm
::::::::::::::::::::::::::::::::::::::

What now?
>GET WORM
OK.
::::::::::::::::::::::::::::::::::::::

What next?
>EXAMINE WORM
Fat and juicy!
::::::::::::::::::::::::::::::::::::::

What next?
>
```

Doreen Bardon is quite well known in adventuring circles through her excellent game helpline services. She's now turned her hand to adventure writing, with the help of Arthur Simmons on the programming side. 'Koosar' was on show at the 2nd Adventure Probe convention where Doreen was looking for a publisher for it. Tony Collins agreed to do the honours and here it is...

The game is 'QUILLed' as you will soon see when you press a key on the intro screen, with the slightly tasteless sub-message 'This game is guaranteed free from AIDS (Adventurer's Instant Death Syndrome)'. Being written using the 'QUILL' it means that all the commands needed are of the VERB-NOUN kind and the game isn't quite as large, or complex, as the average PAWed one.

The intro runs along the lines of this. The night before, you had retired to bed with a book entitled the Fabled Treasure of Koosar. After reading this you go to sleep with the usual dreams of treasure filling your head. When you awake you go for an early morning stroll along the beach. You see something bobbing along among the rocks and decide to investigate...

The thing you find is a bottle. Picking it up isn't as simple as you'd expect, but there's an object lying around nearby that will help you out. Hmm, the bottle appears to be tightly shut so how should you get into it? SMASH BOTTLE succeeds in producing a lot of glass but also the bit of paper that was inside it. But wait, the wind has blown it away! Drat!

Maybe you'll catch up with it later. You have, however, found more interesting things. A quick walk down the pier and you come across a wide gap. By jumping over it you get to a location with a motor boat. Looks like you could have some fun with that, but you'll have to fill it up with petrol and manage to mend the hole in its side first.

Wandering around elsewhere will undoubtedly reveal the fact that the author has missed out a lot of location exits. Also trying SEARCH as well as EXAMINE produces some interesting objects in some places.

There are several stores to visit in the village. The petrol station might help with the boat problem but you'll need some sort of container. 'TOOLS'R'US' has plenty in stock, but the shop assistant won't let you have a look round the storeroom. In the pub is an old sea-dog. Maybe he can help you out, but he doesn't look too happy. How can you cheer him up?

'Koosar' is a good little game, though if it was programmed using the PAW I would've rated it higher. It tends to be a bit unfriendly in the old parser department and would've benefited from the extra memory PAW allows. Even saying that, 'Koosar' isn't a bad example, at all, of a 'QUILLed' game and should contain enough to keep you occupied for a few playing sessions.

Finally, just a quick word about the FREE game on the B-side. 'Birthday Wish' is another 'QUILLed' game in which you must prepare breakfast in bed for the wife! Though it has a rather short time limit, and most of the things you pick up can't be examined, it's a really funny adventure with lots of wry observations. There's plenty of nice touches. For instance, if you've examine the toilet, in the bathroom, then you can't leave the room unless you wash your hands!

Overall, 'Koosar' coupled with 'Birthday Wish' isn't bad value for money at all. As long as you can put up with 'QUILLed' games then they're both worth looking at. You can usually rely on a 'QUILLed' game to give you solid puzzles, rather than the flashy 2-dimensional ones of their PAWed counterparts, and 'Koosar' won't let you down.

You are in your bedroom,which is
decorated in a delicate shade of
pink and cream.
Exit S

You can also see...
a four-poster bed with your wife
sleeping in it
::::::::::::::::::::::::::::::::::::

What now...
>EXAMINE BED
The wife did suggest a water-bed
but you said no as we could.....
DRIFT apart.
::::::::::::::::::::::::::::::::::::

What now...
>

The Fisher King (Spectrum 48K)

Written by Dennis Francombe

Published by Zenobi Software

The legend of King Arthur is a popular theme in adventures. 'The Fisher King' sees Dennis Francombe attempting to twist the idea slightly.

The game is PAWed and comes in two parts, requiring the player to save data to cassette and re-load in order to play part two. The story is relatively straight forward. It was the time of the great festival of 'Pentacost' and the good King had summoned the various Lords and Knights of the land to dine with him at Caerleon. In the middle of this great feast the

Loathly Damsel had appeared and asked for a knight to assist her in her quest. It's here that the game starts.

You take on the role of Perceval, a lowly scullion, who has always wanted to be a knight. Your first decision is whether to volunteer for the task. Mind you, you have to do it anyway, whatever you decide. And so, off you go, with the loathly Damsel on the quest to find the Castle Anfortas.

I'm afraid I'm going to have to say immediately that I didn't like this game. My dislike started with little things, like the first response to the prompt of whether you wish to load a saved position from tape. You can only answer 'YEA' or 'NAY'. It's in keeping with the times, of course, but surely the author could have let you type 'YES' or 'NO' as well?

Then there's the opening 'graphic'. I haven't a clue what it's meant to be (a crown perhaps). Also, some of the location messages don't update themselves. For example, at one point you are blocked by a Knight and are told, quite rightly so, that you 'Cannot go anywhere at present'. However, when the Knight is dead the same message appears, despite the fact that you can now go to the east and west!

Other little things irritated me. One of the "what's next?" prompts caused an annoying space on the input line, before the cursor. On one occasion I entered a location, but instead of the location description I got a message about the shield that was present hanging on a tree. The programming seemed to be very basic. On occasions AUTOG object was used when a PLACE object 254 command would have served the purpose better.

(That's a complaint for any PAW nerds, like me, out there!)

Oh, there's also a maze!

The games logic is a little suspect as well. The opening question 'Do you wish to volunteer for the task?' decides whether you'll get past the first 3 locations or not. The answer you'll need is 'NAY' – but I can see no reason, from reading the text and messages, why this should cause the events that unfold to happen at all and why 'YEA' doesn't have the same effect.

The game does have its good points, but I wasn't particularly encouraged to look for them because of some of the issues I encountered. In some games with the above defects I'd ignore them because if the game was good, but in the case of 'The Fisher King' I'm afraid that any brilliance the game has, doesn't shine through at all.

Not up to the usual high standard of Zenobi, but if you like this era or Dennis Francombe's games then it may be worth checking out.

For Pete's Sake (Spectrum 48K)

Written by Jonathan Scott and Stephen Boyd

Published by Zenobi Software

Jonathan Scott, writing on his own, is usually quite insane, with Stephen Boyd he is slightly more controlled. At least, he was when they last collaborated (in 'Out of The Limelight'). In 'For Pete's Sake' I'm not so sure.

The usual Zenobi information sheet shows signs that the insanity has spread from inside the game itself. One side has the usual blurb written by the Balrog/the authors and the command list. But on the other side is a 'newspaper' front page (created using PCG's Spectrum DTP pack) with some background information about the game contained in it. Teenage humour abounds.

'For Pete's Sake' is a two-part game. Following your commands is Julie Brief who has just got divorced from her husband. Her ex is called Pete and seems to have criminal tendencies as he's been arrested and sent to jail (see the newspaper for more details). I'm really not surprised that old Julie has divorced him!

Part One features Matilda, a familiar character from Scott's other adventures starring Basil Hodgkins. Your character, Julie, works in Matilda's beauty parlour in a very odd shopping mall. The mall is strange due to the local council's money saving idea of merging shops... for example the butcher's shop has been merged with the funeral parlour!

For some reason, you have promised Matilda that you will help her make a pot of her famous stew. Goodness knows why... but at least it gives you a focus for the initial part of the game. Matilda, you see, has not only forgotten the ingredients of her stew but also where she originally got the recipe!

Part two features a bit of breaking and entering that reminded me a bit of Scott Denyer's 'Brian And The Dishonest Politician'. This half of the game is probably not quite as enjoyable as the first part.

'For Pete's Sake' features the same screen presentation that I hated so much in 'Out of The Limelight' so I won't repeat my comments on that. What I will say is that 'For Pete's Sake' is quite an amusing, baffling and ridiculously weird game that forms a fun spin-off, side-adventure set in the Zikov trilogy universe. Scott and Boyd can certainly produce interesting games together and it's nice to see that they have found themselves a very original writing style. If you like your adventures to be serious and reality-bound then give this one a miss. Otherwise it may be worth your while checking it out.

A huge restaurant   000/250

And a supercilious one at that!
They really do assume a "holier-
than-thou" attitude around here,
but then a requirement of the
staff is that they are ordained
priests! It is empty at this
hour. A very rude waiter stands
nearby.

Exit(s) : E.W.SE.
@EXAMINE WAITER
There's nothing more to see.
@TALK TO WAITER
"You look very flirtatious," he
remarks suddenly.
@I
I have nothing at all.
@\

The Four Symbols (Spectrum 48K)

Written by The Grue

Published by FSF Adventures

```
Although it hasn't rained for
weeks the pond is still over
half full, the grass around the
edges worn away with the
constant pounding of feet as
villagers vie for position to
witness the ducking of any
would-be witch. Paths lead NW,
NE, SW and SE. Here you see a
ducking stool.
♥♦(♦♥♦(♦♥♦(♦♥♦(♦♥♦(♦♥♦(♦♥♦(♦♥♦(♦

What do you wish to do next?
♦EXAMINE STOOL
What a fine contraption this is,
sturdily made from the best
quality oak. It has been well
maintained over the years and is
in good working order.

What next?
♦/
```

I had been eagerly awaiting the release of 'The Four Symbols' from F.S.F. software. The game, in its original incarnation, was written and programmed by the infamous 'Adventure Probe' reader 'The Grue' for the Amiga. Now, thanks to the programming talents of Larry 'The Lanky Londoner' Horsfield, Spectrum owners can enjoy the game without having to touch a 16-bit machine. Of course, what was a one-part game on the Amiga has had to be split up into three 48K-sized Speccy sections, but we can live with that, can't we?

The games title page contains the cryptic text – "Soon he will awaken and he will return to his quest and your foul life will once again be in danger of ending suddenly, bloodily, and with you on your knees begging for mercy. Your future is much darker than you think... ".

After puzzling over that, a keypress will clear the screen and ask you if you wish to start from a saved position. If not, you'll be placed in the starting locations set in a village.

```
You find yourself encircled by a
crowd of villagers, all staring
at you intensely.
♦♦(♦♥♦(♦♥♦(♦♥♦(♦♥♦(♦♥♦(♦♥♦(♦♥♦(♦

The crowd confer amongst
themselves for a minute then one
of them steps forward and
speaks.....
"We have reason to believe that
you're the owner of a BLACK CAT!
All of us in the village know
from past experience that only a
Witch, Mage or Sorcerer would
keep such company." He lifts up
the black cat that you saw
outside the burnt down hovel and
asks, "Is this YOUR cat?"

What do you wish to do next?
♠SAY "NO"⟋
```

After wandering around for a while you'll find out that the magical 'Four Symbols' have been stolen and this is why the village is plagued by drought and other such misfortunes. You have to act fast in these first few locations as it is not long before you are accused of witchcraft. The only way out of being drowned to death is by volunteering to go and retrieve the symbols from whoever stole them.

The first few problems are quite straight forward... you shouldn't have too much bother solving them. Typing HELP brings up the strange message of... "The hardest trick is to make it look easy." Really? No doubt that will come in handy later on.

Meanwhile make sure that you leave the village with all the possible items. Remember that small items may get dropped in all the excitement and should be placed in a safe place.

I must admit that I didn't expect to find a bug so early on in the game, but I did. It occurs when you have got the cheese in your pocket and you try to eat it... "Floating on the surface of the pond you see a piece of wood." ... prints up the computer, to which I can only say, "Pardon?" Hmmm... not a good start.

A further bug-ette rears its head in the next section, but it isn't really terminal... it just will confuse you slightly. In this next bit you'll come across a band of grave robbers and it'll take a bit of imaginative thinking to get them to part with some of their loot. If you pay attention to the sign that you'll read on your way... "All that you do this place pass by, remember death for you must die." then you'll find yourself at the resting place of the Emerald symbol – It'll take a fair bit of working out how to get at it, though.

After that, it's not really long before you have to cross over a magic bridge and enter the next part. It's the same sort of format here, as is the next part, but that final third section doesn't contain much gameplay – just realms and realms of end text.

The text throughout the game alternates between serious, descriptive prose and quite amusing, witty responses. It gives the adventure a similar feel to some of the early Infocom titles which mixed the macabre and the hilarious with an amazing amount of success.

For instance, at one point you'll find yourself in a cemetery. An inscription here reads... "In our graveyards with warm winds blowing, there's a great deal of to-ing and fro-ing, But can it be said, That the dead are dead, When their nails and their hair are growing?"

Overall – 'The Four Symbols' is an enjoyable adventure probably best suited to the intermediate level of adventurer.

Grabbed by the Ghoulies! (Spectrum 48K)

Written by Scott Denyer

Published by Delbert the Hamster / FSF Adventures

```
You find yourself stuck in a
damp, dingy cell. The walls are
covered in moss and, due to the
fact that there are no windows,
it is pretty dark. The only
light comes through the bars in
the door.
The door leads north.
~~~~~~~~~~~~~~~~~~~~~~~~~~~~~~~~~~~~~~~~~~~~

*WAIT
While waiting you notice that
the guard at the door has fallen
asleep.

*SEARCH CELL
You search every nook and cranny
in the room, and soon find
something that had previously
escaped your notice...
```

Before Mary Whitehouse writes in to complain, maybe I'd best point out that the titular 'ghoulies' in question are of the supernatural kind, ie. ghosts and spectres and the like, and not... erm... well probably not what first sprung to mind.

'Grabbed By The Ghoulies' is a new adventure by Scott Denyer. It previously surfaced for a short period of time on his Delbert The Hamster label, but now it has been released at bargain price by FSF Software.

Forget the plot, as there really isn't one, just concentrate on the task of getting past all the ghosts and ghouls of the haunted house and its surrounding grounds. First, though, you have to escape from the prison that you've been thrown into. You start off in a seemingly empty cell in what turns out to be a typically hard, FSF adventure game opening puzzle. The secret is to be patient, keep searching, take a break, and do a bit of mindless violence! Although I think this opening sequence is rather hard, it's very clever and you'll feel plenty of satisfaction from working it all out.

Once you're out of the cell you have to tread very carefully in order to avoid the guards. Pretty soon you'll meet up with, and rescue, a curious character called Larry The Dwarf. This guy is very short and talks a hell of a lot! Look out for the humorous sequence involving Larry and the pit near the end of the game... a great answer by Scott to a question posed by his playtester.

Escaping the prison takes a lot of thinking as well, and you descend into a network of underground passages. It's here that you meet your first ghost... though it's possible that it may be more scared of you than you are of it. Whenever a ghost appears there's a nice 'Batman' like 'OO-er!' type sequence.

By now, Larry will be getting on your nerves with his constant talking and he seems, early on, to be no help whatsoever. Down in the passageway a locked door stops progress in one direction, but you can easily ascend to the outside world where you find yourself near a haunted house. It's far too spooky to enter from the outside, but the spade you'll find near here will enable you to get in by going through the locked door in the tunnel. Also nearby is an enchanted forest, although you'll have to get past a spectre to get to it. The solution to this problem is great!

Inside the house there are a lot of conventional puzzles and a lot of unorthodox ones involving the supernatural. There are no prizes for guessing that the cat you find may be useful in getting rid of the viscous dog that blocked your way outside, but how on earth are you going to get it to let you pick it up? What possible use will a vacuum cleaner be... remember 'Ghostbusters'? And how on earth can you get the freezer open when it's frozen shut?

```
You are in what appears to be an
old flower garden. However, any
flowers that lived here moved
away long ago, as the place has
been overrun by weeds.
To the east is a driveway.
You also notice...
A cup.
~~~~~~~~~~~~~~~~~~~~~~~~~~~~~~~~~~~~~~~~~~~~~~~~~~~~~
*I
Things that you have...

Some string.
A key.
A bone.
A sheet. (worn)
A spade.
A cup.
A small saw.
A hose.
A Pot Noodle.

And there's more goings on...
```

Watch out for the man-eating table and various attacks

from other supernatural sources, all of which have unique and refreshingly original solutions... sometimes it pays just to be an outright coward. There are plenty of places to explore and a lot to do, and, although you may be pulling your hair out a lot of the time, you'll be having a lot of fun doing so.

There's not much else I can say without spoiling it for you. The text is the usual Scott Denyer fair... mildly humorous with plenty of tongue in cheek gags, and the presentation and programming is good. I originally saw this game in an early form quite a while ago and I was hooked then. Judging from the people who played the game on one of the DTHS demo-machines at last year's Adventurers' Convention I have no doubt that you'll be hooked too.

Excellent value. Buy it.

The Haunting (Spectrum 48K)

Written by Jason Nicholls

Published by The Elven Adventurers / Northern Underground

'The Haunting' is one of several Elven Adventurers games that have been released by Les Floyd's 'Northern Underground' software label. The Elven Adventurers team, headed by Jason Nicholls, also consists of Julie Nicholls, Judith Woods and Brent Ash for this outing.

This isn't the first time that I've seen 'The Haunting'. It was sent to me quite a number of years back to playtest... but it never actually saw the light of day. So, you can imagine my shock upon loading it up and finding that all the points that I'd made about the presentation, spelling, parser and bugs had been ignored... in fact this version was exactly the same as my playtesting copy. Not a good start...

The basic plot runs as follows. You've accepted a challenge to stay at the 'Damned House', a haunted house located at Ravenshead. If you manage to last the night you'll win a small amount of money... goodness knows what happens if you can't manage to last the night as the gates have been locked so you can't escape even if you want to.

White on black text glares at you as you stand before the 'Damned House'. The typeface is one of the worst I've ever seen used in an adventure with a huge letter 'g' that looks like an overgrown tadpole! After a few spelling mistakes, the exits are listed... not as 'Exits: North, South etc' but just as 'North, south etc' which is a tad confusing. The text itself scrolls upwards and away off the top of the screen, not exactly my favourite method as I prefer the location text to be static, and the location description is normally reprinted should you find anything interesting.

After a bit of exploring outside you venture into the three-story house (with a cellar) which is described very vividly, but any atmosphere that may be created by the text is marred by several spelling and grammatical errors. 'There' is often used instead of 'their' and tenses are sometimes mixed up so that words like 'placed' become 'place'.

As for the game itself... well it's not too bad at all, I suppose. The author has got around the very un-original plot by including several interesting puzzles. The novel use of a pendant as a help command is very good. There are plenty of encounters with demons and the like, and you'll even find yourself at the gateway to Hell at one point in the game.

The parser copes with most things you throw at it although at one point the rather obscure FEEL IN MIRROR needs to be used where I think that TOUCH MIRROR would have done the job just as well. EXAMINE can be abbreviated to X, but not EXAM. Also RS/RL for RAMSAVE/RAMLOAD can't be used... which is off-putting as these are standard these days.

The Haunting is a very uneven game. It has some interesting ideas, but the overall experience is marred by the inclusion of a lot of very familiar puzzles and one of the oldest plots in the book.

A Holiday to Remember (Spectrum 48K)

By Trevor Taylor

Published by Visual Dimensions / The Guild

'A Holiday to Remember' is one of the three Visual Dimension titles that The Guild have re-released recently. It's a two-part text adventure, with a smattering of graphics, PAWed by Trevor Taylor. However, unlike the other Visual Dimension games this one doesn't get off to too good a start.

The plot, for instance, seems a little suspect. You play Malcolm Wright-Nutter who has just been sent to take a holiday with his eccentric uncle at his house in Crockham-by-Sea. You arrive at the bus stop but your uncle is nowhere to be seen. What has happened to him?

You soon find out when you come across his burnt down house. Though how it's burnt down seems to be a mystery! In the ruins of the house you find a strange torch-like device and a Gatling gun.

There are other places to visit such as the garage and the shed (where a nasty discovery awaits you!) and then there's the town itself.

The town is populated by an amazing three people (you can only do something with two of them) a policeman, a shopkeeper and a cinema attendant, and these characters inhabit what is certainly the most boring town I've ever been in.

But you're wondering just what is so 'suspect' about the plot, aren't you? Well, early on you come across a statue that when pushed (several times) it reveals a gap in its base which you can enter. On doing so you find yourself in an old mine where there's a big hole that leads down to Australia!

Overall though, if you can manage to suspend your disbelief to enjoy this very surreal adventure, 'Holiday' isn't that bad of an experience. There are, however, a few too many useless objects and locations in the game. If you want to try one of the Visual Dimension games – then try 'Reality Hacker', which I enjoyed a lot more.

Homicide Hotel (Spectrum 48K)

Written by James Bentley

Published by Wallsoft / The Guild

'Homicide Hotel' is a detective game by James Bentley. You play John Stafford, a private investigator who has been called in by the local police to help solve a baffling murder that took place in a hotel in Knightford.

The murder in question is that of Mr Andrews (a famous film star) and it's not long before you discover from the doctor staying at the hotel that old Agatha Christie's favourite, strychnine was used. In fact, the doctor tells you that some of the substance is missing from his bag. Could he have done it?

The game starts off with you wandering round the hotel looking for the various suspects and questioning them about their alibis. The chief suspect is Mr Andrews new wife – Ms Carmel Emeldra. But, as we all know from TV detective shows, the obvious suspect never did it. Or maybe she did.

But that's for you to find out by asking questions and exploring the hotel. The method of conversation is very long winded. To ask a character about their alibi you must type SAY TO CHARACTER "TELL ME ABOUT YOUR ALIBI" and the same goes for most other topics. I would have preferred a shorter ASK CHARACTER ABOUT ALIBI type command. It's no fun to type in the longer winded version again and again.

You're not limited to exploring just the hotel, the town of Knightford can also be investigated, which is vital for checking out alibis, as is the use of a telephone.

Overall, this is probably one of the most successful attempts at a detective game that I've played with only the speech routine letting it down. The occasional graphics gain the game extra brownie points.

I Dare You! (Spectrum 48K)

By Louise Wenlock (Anthony Collins)

Published by The Guild

'I Dare You!' is the latest 'Pegasus Software' game from 'The Guild'. Unlike the previous 'Pegasus' games this one's been written by a new adventure author – Louise Wenlock. The strange thing about the game is that, apart from the cassette tape, the game box also includes three little sealed envelopes. So, what are they for?

That was exactly the very question I was asking myself when I loaded up the game and read through the introductory text. The story starts with you, (be you male or female) at a get-together of adventure players in Birmingham, talking to your friend Lizzie. You tell her that you wish you could play a real adventure in the real world, for once, instead of on your computer. With a smile she informs you that this might well be possible! She tells you that she has a relation who has a huge mansion outside Birmingham that she could borrow. She says that she will set up a challenge inside it for you. You don't take her seriously – after all, she's well known for her practical jokes – but when she dares you to go, you decide to take up the challenge.

And that is where the game begins. I found myself in my own house, but there weren't any little envelopes in sight. There was, however, a letter on my doormat. Pausing only to admire the neat presentation in the game, I picked this up and examined it. After ripping it open I found a few objects inside. There was a letter from Lizzie, which told me that the key to the house was enclosed, together with some money to pay for a cab to get there. She hadn't told me the address, but had enclosed a small pink card with a clue to the name of the road on it.

Examining the card provided the response 'See the games packaging!' And, lo and behold, one of the little envelopes was marked 'Pink Card'. Ripping it open gave me a pink card with a cryptic clue on it. It didn't prove too difficult to solve and I soon found myself at Lizzie's relation's mansion (using the taxi rank near my house).

Once inside I found a whole host of objects. The good thing was that I could carry as much as I liked. A cryptic message on the telephone read 'Keep Safe: 021-749-1111', I wondered what it meant. A huge gate blocked the staircase – I would need to find a key to open that, I bet.

Exploring additional rooms in the mansion, I found that most of the problems were of the 'down to earth' kind. All the objects are well hidden. Everything in sight must be examined, and the whole feel of the game reminded me very much of a 'Linda Wright' adventure (which is no bad thing).

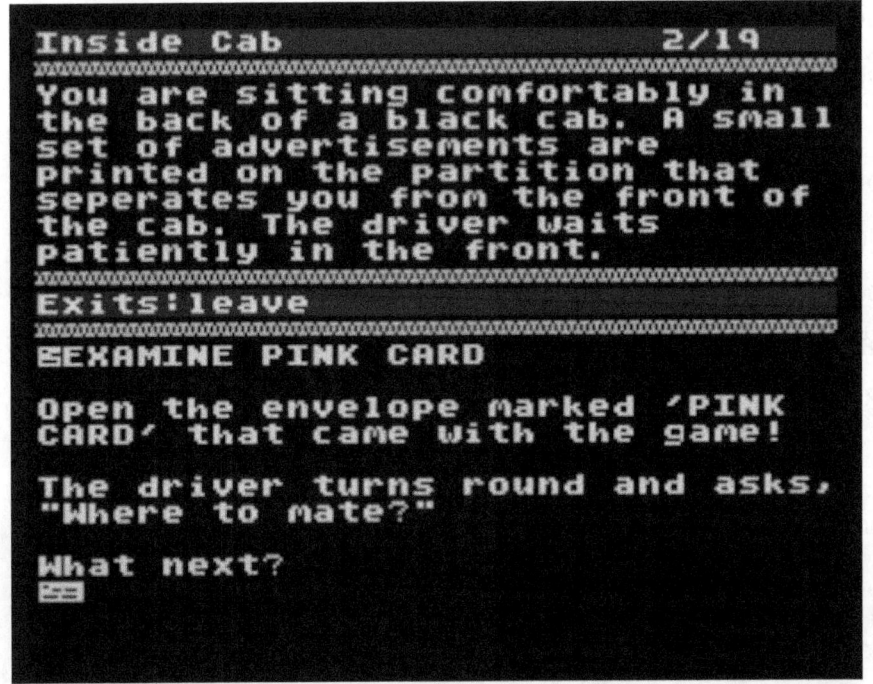

Strangely enough, the task of getting up the stairs involved building a model car. It was scattered in bits all over the house, and, as well as assembling it, I had to find and mend a remote control unit. All this was good fun – I had to throw boomerangs and do some hoovering up. In a few places the logic of the game seemed a bit suspect, but it was mostly spot on and you could imagine an adventure like this actually being constructed in the real world.

Once up the stairs, the game continued in the same sort of manner. What was good was that in virtually every game location there is a 'cryptic' HELP message. Well done, Louise, for putting them in.

The envelopes form a real incentive – You will desperately want to get onto the next section just so you can rip open the things and see what's on the cards inside!

'I Dare You!' is a good little game full of neat little puzzles. No flashy features or effects, but good, solid, adventuring fun. For £2.50 it's worth checking out. As an extra bonus there is a 128K demo of Tony Collins' next adventure 'Absolution' (The sequel to the excellent 'The Hermitage') on the B-side.

Jester's Jaunt (Spectrum 48K)

Written by June Rowe with Paul Cardin

Published by Zenobi Software

Unusually, for me, I'm going to start the review by telling you a bit about the authors. Paul Cardin (the programmer) is the author of the 'classic' spectrum sci-fi tale, 'Captain Kook', and June Rowe (the designer) is one of the Spectrum's best play-testers. So, what do you get when a top programmers and playtester join forces? A pretty good game, that's what!

You are the youngest member of your family of six brothers. Christened 'Early' by your father, who had a brilliant sense of humour, you are the Royal Jester of the court. Life is grand, the Prince and Princess are kind to you and all their other servants, amongst them your six brothers. In fact, you all had a peaceful and happy life – That was, until the evil Witch Vilana kidnapped the Prince!

And guess what? You are the one who has to go and rescue him; your other brothers are busy working in the palace. But you aren't sent empty handed. No, indeed not, for your brothers will each give you a gift of some sorts. There's just one little problem. You'll need to say goodbye to them, by name, before they'll give you the gifts. "How is that difficult?", you may ask. Well, the thing is – You've called them by their nicknames for so long that you can't remember their real names. Oh well, you know that they're named after the first six letters of the greek alphabet and that there's a book on the subject in the library. Maybe that'll help you remember the name of the princess too, for she also has a gift for you. Oh, by the way; the library door is locked.

And so, you start wandering round the grounds of the palace. After exchanging a few words with the sentry you're told that you won't be allowed to leave until you've got all the necessary objects. A quick swim in the pond helps you find a key – but unfortunately your clothes get drenched through. Unless you find a way to dry them, you'll die of pneumonia.

There are plenty of animals to help you with your adventure. A dog may well become your best friend, if you've got something tasty to bribe him with. There's also the pony that you'll need to ride. Unfortunately, he seems rather scared of you.

```
You are in an annexe off the
entrance hall, where citizens
await an audience with the
prince.
Exits NE W
```

```
Your brother, Brains, appears,
whispers in your ear "Even if
you don't know what to do with
anything, don't throw it away.
You might need it later" then
leaves.
*I
You have: nothing.

You are wearing: a jester's
suit.
```

Objects, characters and magic lie around every corner in 'Jester's Jaunt'. Even the gifts your brothers give you have mysterious uses! The text is a sheer delight to read. It's descriptive and sometimes humorous, with very good characterisations of the various creatures you'll come across in your quest. Should you die, you'll be treated to some of June's poetry – Read it carefully, there's bound to be a few hints in it somewhere.

Presentation is good, with a clear font and plenty of colour. The usual commands and abbreviations are present, X for EXAMINE, RL for RAMLOAD etc.

Altogether a highly polished and crafted game with so many good features that I have to recommend it. In fact, I could go on and on about it, though you'll be thankful to hear that I won't.

I will, however, tell you that it comes in two PAWed parts. The second of which requires saved data from part one, though you're allowed to have a look around without any data (to see what you're up against).

Summing up – A great game. I look forward for another from June and Paul in the not too distant future.

Sadly, June never did go on to write another Spectrum adventure. She was a well-loved and active member of the adventuring scene, having written for fanzines like Adventure Probe, From Beyond and the Spectrum Adventurer tapezine. She also contributed to the development of countless adventures through her work as a playtester.

Leotrope (Spectrum 48K)

Written by Graham Burtenshaw

Published by Graham Burtenshaw / Delbert the Hamster
Software

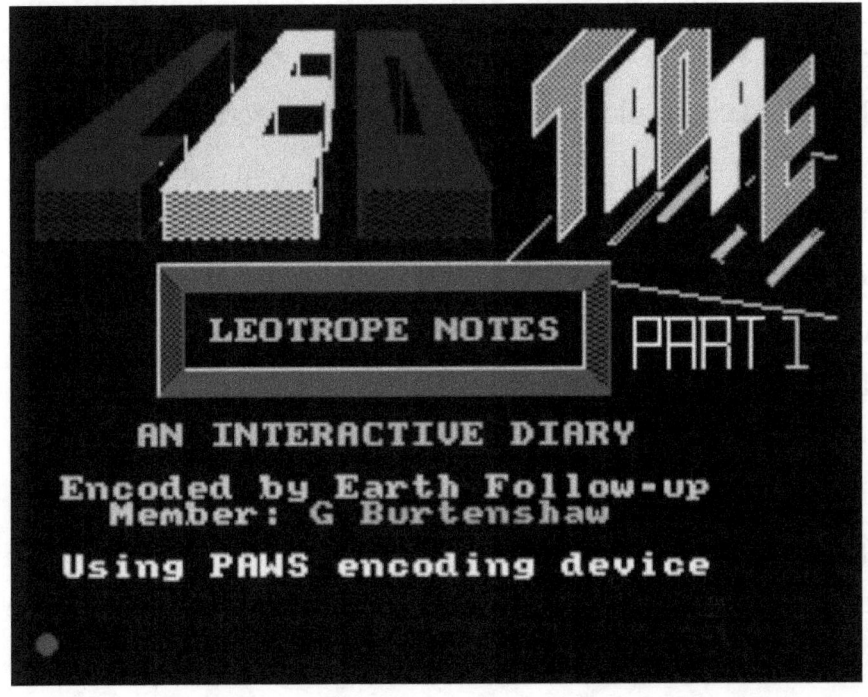

Constructed from the recollections of Traun Nuronion Baker, 'Leotrope' is a two-part interactive diary encoded by Earth follow-up member Graham Burtenshaw using the PAW encoding system. Or at least that's what the title pages tell you when you load up the game and far be it for me to contradict them and call it a 'sci-fi' adventure from the editor of Enceladus.

Whatever title you give it, the plot remains the same. Your name is Nuronion Baker, a citizen of Leo-Lantis, and you are an alien. Without the knowledge of the natives of planet Earth, your people have been studying them and flying to and from the planet for years. However, recently a routine flight to Earth encountered difficulties and crash landed. Unfortunately, some of the humans witnessed this and this caused a great threat to the security of the mission. Your task is simple journey to Earth, reclaim the gravity controller that was housed in the ship and destroy all the information about the crash.

You start in your house and soon your boss, Narodion Jones, summons you to the airport. It's evident at this stage that you definitely should NOT do as your told as there are plenty of rooms to explore first in your house and even an attic... if you can find it.

Graham has created a very weird and quite amusing alien civilisation with all sorts of strange gadgets and gizmos. There are several native creatures, as well, such as the barmin and the fafool. Then there are the poor old wacaboos. Not only do the inhabitants eat these poor defenceless creatures and use them as slaves in their vending machines, but they also use them as a source of light. Yes, these creatures will glow when excited, so the population put them in lamps and passes an electric current through them! Apparently one wacaboo will last up to 6 months without food, after that you'll need to replace it with a new one. Just don't tell the RSPCA-liens!

But back to the apartment. You really do need to explore it thoroughly – advice which you should keep in mind for all locations in the game. You need to EXAMINE ON and UNDER everything. FEEL UNDER things. LOOK IN things. The command WORN may even be useful. Plus, you have to SEARCH some locations as well... and sometimes SEARCH things WELL. (Though it is obvious when you will need to do this)

```
This is a foul smelling part of
the attic system, about two
houses away from your own.
Despite the myths that Trauns
have exceptional levels of
hygeine, there are several
'Ienisins' running about. There
is a wall to the south.

You notice :
An iron needle

ꟽꟽꟽꟽꟽꟽꟽꟽꟽꟽꟽꟽꟽꟽꟽꟽꟽꟽꟽꟽꟽꟽꟽꟽꟽꟽꟽꟽꟽꟽꟽꟽꟽꟽ

What is Nurodion to do?
▪➤GET NEEDLE
You now have the iron needle.

Now what?
▪➤✕
```

After exploring the apartment it's into your travel balloon and on to the airport. Again – don't do as you're told and follow Jones, make sure you explore the rest of the town and the airport terminal as well first.

Part one ends when you are on Earth. Part two requires a password and involves you trying to get back the device and destroy the information. This part has more conventional puzzles in it. There's also a 'maze' in this bit, but you'll have no problems with it if you remember that there are other directions apart from N, S, E and W.

Overall, 'LEOTROPE' is quite enjoyable. I know that the author doesn't think much of it, but I find that it gave a few hours of good adventuring. Decidedly different... and that's a compliment.

Graham Burtenshaw authored three Spectrum adventures ('Leotrope', 'Cell of the Ridges' and 'Doomsday'). He is perhaps better known for his work in the Sam Coupe community where he produced the Enceladus magazine, designed hardware, wrote the game Momentum and created the highly-regarded SAM Paint software.

The Lost Dragon! (Spectrum 48K)

By Tom Frost

Published by Tartan Software

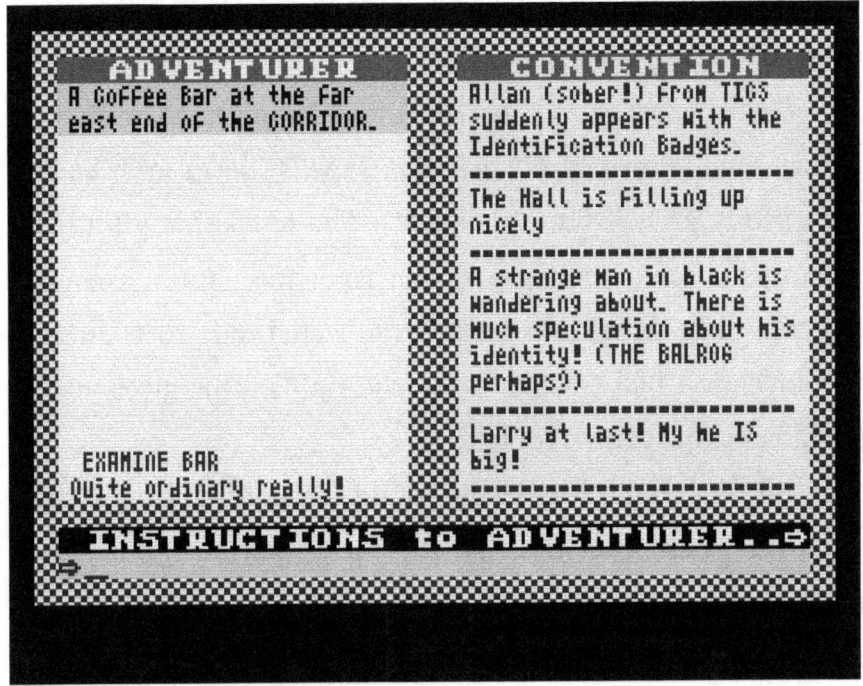

'The Lost Dragon' isn't exactly a new game, but it's Tom Frost's most recent game on his Tartan label. I got my copy at the 2nd Adventure Probe Convention in an effort to find out exactly what went on the first time around...

On loading the game, I was greeted with the now familiar Tartan split-screen display. Because, for once, I'd read the instructions I could tell that on the right was an uncontrollable adventurer standing in the convention hall, whilst I was on the left. Confused? Ahem – well here's the plot...

Basically, a wizard has snaffled the dragon trophy due to be presented at the awards ceremony and it's up to you to get it back. For some strange reason the wizard lives on the third floor of the hotel (maybe they offer good rates to spellcasters?) and it's that floor that you'll have to enter if you want to have any chance of getting the dragon back.

The wizard gives you a bit of a helping hand himself in the form of a telepathic pill and three spells (never let it be said that wizards aren't sporting chaps!). The telepathic pill proves rather useful as you grab a poor unsuspecting punter, shove the pill down their throat and get them to watch the proceedings in the convention hall (displayed on the right). This gives you an idea of how long you've got left.

So off you go, wandering round the hotel until you come to the lift where you find that there's no button for the third floor. Hmm... You also find a rather nifty looking box outside, but the doorman won't let you enter the hotel with it!

There are plenty of locations to explore, with several rooms, floors and even the infamous bar! To make things easier on the mapping you're given the option of entering the EXPLORE mode which stops the clock and allows you to waltz around to your hearts content. You can't actually GET anything in this mode though, but it's very useful.

As you'd expect in a Tartan game, the emphasis is on devious problems rather than brilliant text. The responses tend to be a bit short and abrupt half the time and the examine messages leave a lot to be desired. But all that is more than made up for by the rather witty 'Convention Report'. Familiar names keep cropping up and I've played the game several times just to read the goings on in the convention hall!

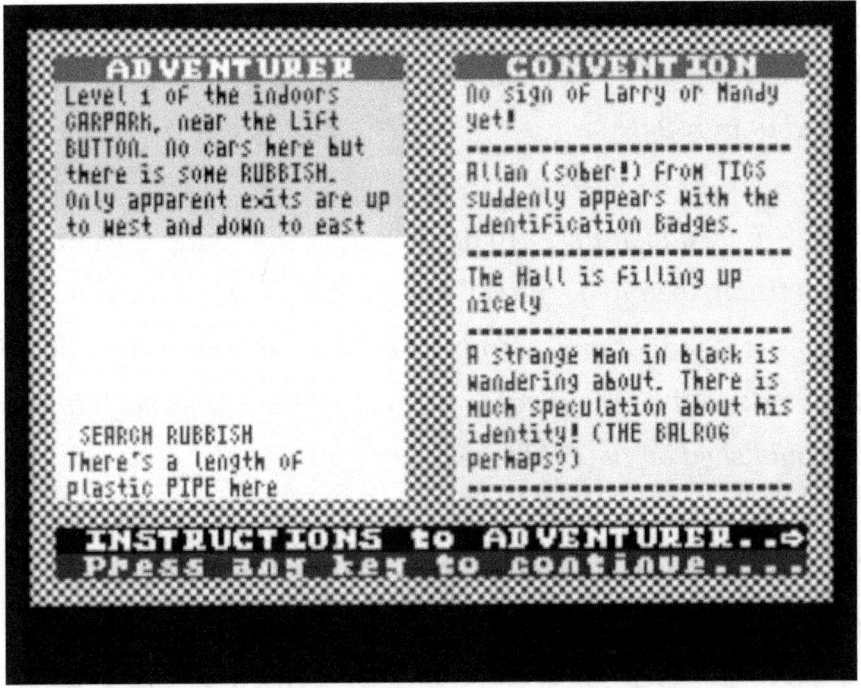

Tom Frost has made a name for himself through producing solid puzzle filled adventures and 'The Lost Dragon' is a perfect example of his games and as such should be enjoyed by all ages of players.

At the 2nd Probe Convention Tom Frost warned that he might just 'spill the beans' on that times 'get together' – Let's hope that many a true word is said in jest and that he does. Come on Tom, Write another!

One of Tom Frost's early adventuring claim to fames was that he was the winner of Incentive's Mountain of Ket Trilogy competition, being the first adventurer in the UK to 100% all three parts of that challenging game series. His efforts landed him the prize of a £400 video recorder... Not a prize to be sniffed at in 1985!

Tom's first adventure, '1942 Mission' also has links to a competition, being a runner-up for the Sinclair User/Cases Computer Simulations 'Cambridge Award'. Not only did he receive £250 for his submission (top prize was £2000!), it was also published on the CCS label.

Tom's excellent programming skills were soon put to use on the games he released on his Tartan Software imprint. He produced his own 'Adventure Builder Software' and a whole selection of games, including the excellent 'Door' series that are a great starting point for anyone new to the hobby.

The Magic Isle (Spectrum 48K)

By Palmer P. Eldritch (Richard Hewison)

Published by Zenobi Software

'The Magic Isle' is the sequel to 'A Legacy for Alaric'. The game sets off where the first one ended, so it's pretty vital that you've played the first one. In case you haven't, Zenobi have thoughtfully included a copy on the B-side of the tape.

You play an adventurer (you shouldn't have too much bother roleplaying that) who has been set the task of rescuing some poor prat called Alaric, just so he can claim his legacy.

The game starts with you in a rowing boat surrounded by a huge array of objects (the ones you had to collect in the first game!). It's a little overwhelming to have so many objects available at the start of the game, especially when you're an adventurer who's used to starting with nothing, but you can luckily stuff them in a very large (and useful) bag that the author has thoughtfully provided, until you're ready to take them all in.

And so, you leave the boat and wander about the island where the adventure takes place. The game is very tongue-in-cheek and humorous. You come across a staff stuck in some sand and when you try to take it you are told that 'it's difficult getting staff these days'! Elsewhere, you find a ladder which is black in colour and are informed that it had a TV series named after it. Then there's a statue of a spellcaster made out of sand – Yes, it's a 'sand witch'. When you try to eat it you are told, 'You can't do that, but at least you got the joke.'

As you progress further in the game, you'll encounter killer-butterflies, an incredibly intelligent sword and rope, and a very weird mug. Watch out for the rather scary hands which come up from the ground and grab at your legs!

'The Magic Isle' wasn't quite my cup of tea but if you treat it as a two-part game (as that's what you basically get on the tape) then I don't think you'll be disappointed with your purchase. I look forward to playing the next Palmer P. Eldrich game, if only to see in what direction he takes his humour.

The Magician's Apprentice (Spectrum 48K)

Written by Simon Avery

Published by The Guild

```
    You're in a slight widening of
the EAST-WEST path. The forest
borders either side and prevents
any movement in that direction.

A small and brightly coloured
Demon jumps out from the under-
growth and stands in the middle
of the road, blocking any way
West.

Wunty awaits.
▮EXAMINE DEMON

He seems to be quite agitated at
your presence and hops from one
foot to the other squeaking
nervously.

Wot now mush?
>
```

"Hello there! My names Wuntvar. What d'ya mean, "That's a stupid name?' You should hear the name of my master, the magician Ebeneezum. Now, isn't that something to laugh at? And you know what? He's only gone and got himself lost somewhere. Being the helpful sort of chap I am I'm going to go and look for him, and you're going to help me. Okay?

Yes, This is my hut. Not much to look at, I know, what with the roof having fallen through and the crumbling walls, but it's home to me. No, I don't mind if you call me 'Wunty' – after all, the prompt does. Yes, that BACKPACK and STAFF do look interesting. Okay – I'll EXAMINE the BACKPACK. Oh look, I've found something. What d'ya mean, "What is it?" Type 'LOOK' and see. Yes, I know it's a pain but that's the way it is in this adventure. Okay?

What do YOU want to do now? Oops, sorry. I've just suffered a mild identity crisis. It must be the fact that all the prompts ask you to give directions to me, and yet most of the responses are as though YOU'VE carried out the actions. I don't wish to complain, but surely I deserve some credit for it?

Oh, so we're going for a walk now, are we? Oh great, We've come across a DEMON. What d'ya mean, "HIT HIM"?. What if I die? No, I can't RAMSAVE you twit – That command is sadly absent from this adventure. Okay, Okay – I'll hit the dratted thing. Well, that's got rid of the wimp hasn't it?

I think I'll just wander about a bit now. Yes, that's right, I'm taking control now. Oh, my goodness! I've got lost in a maze. Any ideas? Ple-a-se! 'READ MAP'? Good idea.. Great, I'm out of the maze and in the house of my true love Norrie. Excuse me for a minute, will you? What d'ya mean, "Cut that out, you've got your master to rescue!!" Can't I just give her one peck on the cheek. Spoil sport! Okay, I'll save the kissing till later.

I'll just pop upstairs and see Norrie's gran. Okay, I'll EXAMINE her BED (If you really want me to). Oh look, I've found something. Funny place to find a top-hat. Curiously, as well, Granny doesn't mind me looking around. Mind you she's too busy insulting me. What, you want to know what she's saying? Oh, just something about me not being good enough for Norrie and how I'm off chasing after an old busy-body wizard who can't even find his own hat in the mornings. Wait a sec', did she say hat? So that's who it belongs to!

```
 You're in a slight widening of
the EAST-WEST path. The forest
borders either side and prevents
any movement in that direction.
I can also see:-
A small angry Demon.

Tell me.
>EXAMINE DEMON
He seems quite agitated at your
presence and hops from one foot
to the other squeaking nervously

Wot now mush ?
>I
I have with me:-
A backpack.
A map.
A sturdy Oak Staff.

Wot now mush ?
>
```

'QUIT'? You're not going already are you? What do you mean, you've gotta write a review? That's a feeble excuse if ever I heard one! Aha, so you want ME to tell you what else is in the game, eh? Okay... Well being 'QUILLed' it's not super huge, but what is there is humorous and quite well designed. I mean, I've come across things like dragons, maidens, a warrior with a war club and a strange character called Grax. Plus I've been talking to trees and sneezing quite a lot! I mean, what more could you ask for?

What? Yes, I do recommend it to adventurers. I mean, it's a nice little game for a couple of quid and should keep them busy for a few days. As an added bonus, you get to guide me around! Is that it then? Any last commands before you go? You what?!! I think I'll reset for that – Go wash your mouth out with soap!!"

Simon Avery, also sometimes writing under the pseudonym Michael Hunt, was a prolific author of Amstrad CPC and ST adventures. Both The Guild and The Adventure Workshop converted many of his adventures to the Spectrum, and WoW Software produced Commodore 64 versions. Always well-designed, and often humorous, Simon's games are well worth checking out on any format.

Marooned (Spectrum 48K)

Written by Laurence Creighton

Published by Zenobi Software

There are some things that it's a good idea to be able to do if you want to do certain jobs in life. If you're going to be a pilot, then it would probably be a good idea to have a basic knowledge how a parachute works (as well as how to fly a plane). If you're going to be a sailor, then maybe it would be a good idea to learn how to swim...

Not so with the guy you've taken over the role of in 'Marooned'. This is one chap who hasn't really taken his own safety into consideration. He's built a yacht, took it out for trials and hasn't thought about wearing a life-jacket... this guy can't swim, for goodness sake. Needless to say, your starting position isn't too good as you've just been hit by a storm that's wrecked your yacht and has thrown you out into the cold sea with only a ladder to keep you company (no, I don't know how it got there either!)

```
You are floundering in the icy
sea.   The wind is howling about
you and the waves are as big as
houses.   Your yacht has been
wrecked, the horizon seems like
a million miles, and there is no
sign of land.

YOU NOTICE:
A fin swimming towards you

*EXAMINE FIN
It belongs to a dolphin.

*RIDE DOLPHIN
Riding on the dolphin's back,the
animal takes you to the shore of
an uncharted island. It drops
you on the beach, and with a
wave of its flipper swims back
out to sea.
```

Luckily a passing dolphin can see you back on dry land... if you can manage to coax the parser to move you onto it. Once you've been rescued, you'll find yourself on a desert island without even your favourite records to keep you company. Once past the first obstacle (a use for the ladder!) you'll encounter the natives of this island who'll need quite a bit of thought to get past correctly. You'll also need their help later on.

The local inhabitants don't seem to be the only people who have set foot on the island. There's a large laboratory that's quite well protected and you'll need to get in there at some point.

You definitely have to watch the order you do things in this game as once you've done certain things you'll be unable to do others. There's more than one way of solving a problem, a trick Laurence uses quite often, and you'll usually find that if you can solve a problem immediately when you first find it then you've solved it in the wrong way.

The game was written using the 'QUILL' and has quite reasonable presentation. The story doesn't hang together too well as it seems just an excuse for the author to link together certain puzzles... but then that's where Laurence's games have their strength, in the puzzles, so suspend belief for a while and get the thinking cap on for some serious adventuring.

Methyhel (Spectrum 48K & 128K)

Written by Anthony Collins

Published by Zenobi Software / The Guild

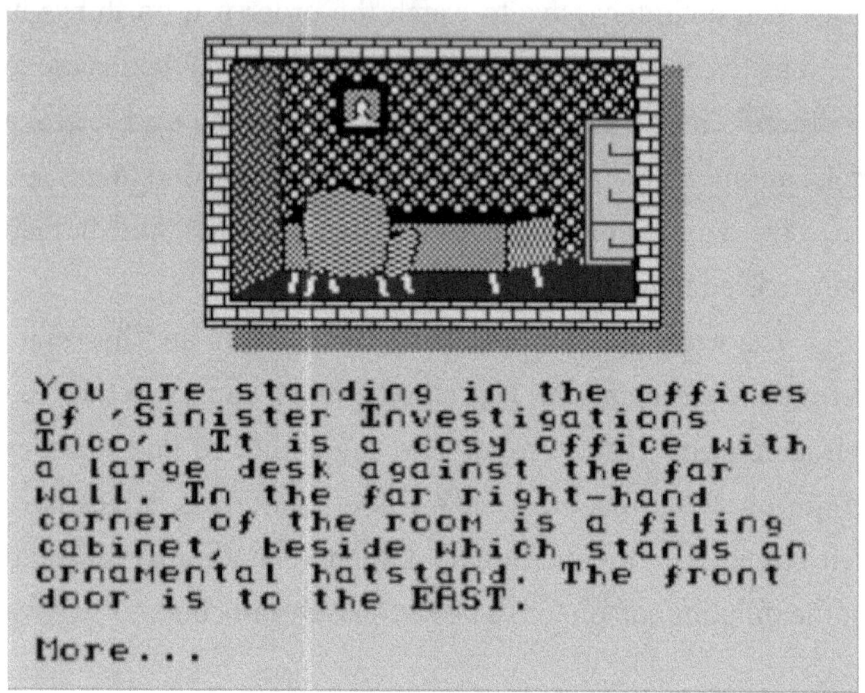

First the facts – Methyhel is an updated version of Tony Collins' Amstrad adventure game, Nethyhel. There are two versions available for the Spectrum; the two-part 48K version, originally released by Zenobi, and a 'Special Edition' 128K version which Tony made available on his own The Guild label.

Methyhel opens up in the offices of Sinister Investigations Inc, where you, Professor Jack Slaine (the head of SI) have just received a mysterious telegram from a Doctor Morgan asking you to come to his house immediately. SI doesn't investigate the usual things, like cheating spouses, but rather the paranormal and occult. As you can imagine, the mystical amulet enclosed with the telegram interests Jack Slaine greatly.

Before attempting to leave the office, you should note that examining the office itself produces several useful objects including a coat and the all-important wallet full of folding green stuff. Your secretary is also in the nearby computer room and can give quite a bit of help if you ask here the right questions.

Then it's out into the cold streets of London where a conveniently placed taxi rank provides a useful way of getting about. There are various places you can visit, but at first you won't know where to head for, so it's best to check out the Doc's house first.

Once there you will have your first encounter with the supernatural in the form of a huge demonstalker, who stands over Morgan's dead body and isn't too friendly at all! Now may be a good time for a note on the spell system!

The spells come in the form of three words, written on an object. You need to carry the object in order to focus the spell. A neat idea but despite the supernatural elements it was a little disappointing that the spells don't really play a major part in the game until near the end.

The main feature of the game is the amount of travelling you do via various modes of transport. The locations you visit follow logically on from each other and you can double back and revisit places if you wish. Eventually you end up in France, where the root of the problem lies, and it requires a cunning bit of spell manipulation to defeat Methyhel, I can tell you.

My only criticisms of the original 48K version where the breakdown in logic in some places and unused locations in part two. However, the 128K version sees a tighter plot, more puzzles, better programming and the whole thing crammed into one load. You do lose the graphics; a small price to pay, though.

Overall, Methyhel is a good paranormal investigation game. It is well worth checking out; particularly the 128K version.

As well as authoring many highly regarded games, such as The Hermitage and Theseus and the Minotaur, Tony Collins ran The Guild software label. He was responsible for converting a large number Amstrad and Commodore titles so they could be enjoyed by Spectrum adventurers.

The Mines of Lithiad (Spectrum 48K)

Written by Jack Lockerby

Published by Zenobi Software

Like clockwork, Jack Lockerby continues to produce one top notch adventure every two months. This time the title is 'The Mines of Lithiad', the publisher is Zenobi, the price £2.49... But what of the game itself?

Cavilan was angry, and when a giant dragon gets angry you don't really want to be around! Mind you, the anger is quite understandable really. I mean, if you were the last of the dragons, because some evil blighter had killed all the others, and that same evil blighter had pinched your egg in the hope that you would come after it and he could clobber you as well, then you'd probably be quite annoyed as too!

Cavilan may be a dragon but she isn't a fool. She knows that there's no way that she's going to be able to get her egg back herself, so she looks to the dragon-riders for help. She chooses you to go on the quest to get back her egg and tells you to wait by her cave on Silvertooth Mountain while she goes and does one or two things.

And so that's where the game starts, atop Silvertooth Mountain. As usual, for Jack, the game is PAWed and has his easy to read font. Unusually, the input line appears at the bottom of the screen which can be confusing at first.

After WAITing for Cavilan to arrive you're taken to Kalam wood and she tells you that there's a mine due south of your current position which leads to an old worm trail. After wondering round and noticing the odd lightning FX you'll discover that Jack has made maximum use of locations and memory by having one location representing a whole set of actual game locations by using flags to change your 'position' and alter the possible exits. Jack also used this approach in 'The Bounty Hunter' to good effect.

Due to the fact that the locations are all similar, careful mapping is essential, especially later on in the game when you enter the mines themselves.

After some exploring, you'll come across the body of an old man lying across the trail. Whether he's dead or alive when you find him depends on how long you've taken to reach his position. He's dying of thirst, you see, so it's essential that you get some water to him quick. But how? The well in the old well house is working perfectly, but the bucket has a hole in it.

As well as the well house there's another hut across the river. EXAMining the bed reveals a lamp, but you'll need a flint to get it. Being more specific about where you EXAMine will reveal a jug as well which will help you with the problem of the old man.

It pays to WAIT in a certain place, but only once you've EXAMined a certain thing mentioned in the location text, this will get you a spade which proves useful and should reveal something that is some help with the lamp problem.

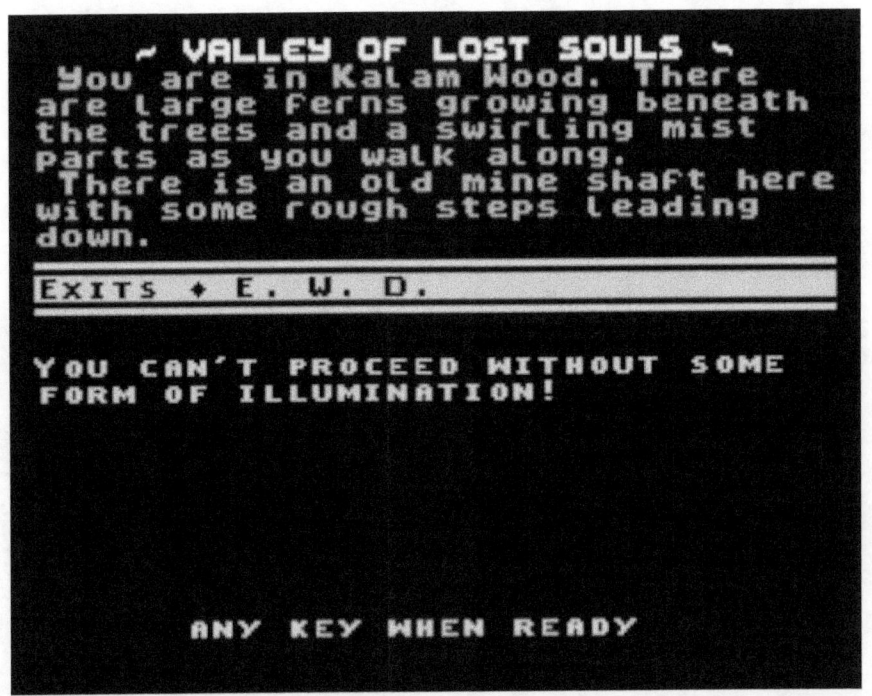

147

Then it's down into the mine itself. The first thing you'll encounter is a bridge. It does have a gap in it, but you can jump it... just don't expect to get back! Then it's onto a weaving winding array of tunnels. Take my advice and map this carefully as there are about four or five locations that you should visit.

There's a maximum of four objects that can be carried at once, so you have to think carefully about what you carry and what you leave behind in the various stages of the game. By the time you encounter the turtle you will have scored about 30%.

After then things really start getting interesting as you race to get the egg back to Cavilan before you are discovered... plenty of action in this bit, and a lot of subterfuge is necessary.

To sum it up, another great title from Lockerby... not quite as good as 'The Dark Tower' but well worth looking out for!

Murder He Said (Spectrum 128K)

Written by Jack Lockerby

Published by Zenobi Software

I've always been one for a good old detective yarn with lots of dead bodies, loads of suspects, an unorthodox detective and a final (completely illogical) plot twist that makes the murderer someone who had supposedly died ten years earlier, which is probably why I was looking forward to 'Murder He Said'. That, and the fact that it was written by Jack Lockerby.

You take on the role of Inspector Vance and must solve the murder of Philip Stowe. He was found dead at Dundee Manor, the home of Major Dundee and his nut cake of a wife.

So, who is Philip Stowe?

The answer to that lies within the pages of the casebook that your trusty sergeant has prepared for you. It contains some incredibly useful information about all the people at the house where the murder was committed. To read the entries all I had to do was type FILE ON so and so, and then it was up to me and my 'little grey cells' to do the rest.

```
INSIDE A POLICE STATION
You are inside a police station
standing next to a desk. Behind
the desk sits a sergeant. A
short corridor leads north and
the door to the street is south.
................................................
Exits:- N, S,
................................................
The sergeant is here.
TALK TO SERGEANT
"Excuse me Sir, but aren't you
supposed to be investigating a
murder. You wont solve much by
talking to me, will you?"
I
You are carrying some keys, a
casebook and a bleeper.
And you are wearing a suit.
```

Looking around in the starting location didn't yield many clues... probably because I started off in my office. On the side I found a nice little bleeper that I could use to call my constable when I wanted some object tested or needed someone to buy me a pint. The car keys I found here weren't for the red Jaguar outside but for the small green Skoda. On my way out, I passed the Chief Constable's office and heard Abba music coming from within... no wonder they call him Strange.

Once I arrived at Dundee Manor I had a quick look round the grounds and met up with the very suspicious gardener, planting evidence perhaps? A look through the household rubbish produced some nice blue gloves... I decided that if I found out who they belonged to I'd ask them for the pattern; they'd make such a nice gift for my nephew Raymond.

Elsewhere I found something even more interesting and I decided that now was the time to make my grand entrance. Excuse me, Sir, I'm from the police.

I was met by Major Dundee himself, who my wife (that's Mrs. Vance) is a great fan of. He left to go and comfort his own wife and I was free to explore the house and barge in without anybody complaining about search warrants. I had been informed of the names of all the cast in the opening titles and so I went round QUESTIONing them all.

Once I had collected their statements I quickly realised that something didn't add up. It's a shame I hadn't brought my pocket calculator. When I found an item, I could SHOW it to various people or GIVE it to my constable to go and get analysed. The reports were speedily processed and placed on the table in the hallway for me (and any passing criminal) to read.

I could also FOLLOW people around and even LISTEN at keyholes. Thank goodness Hastings wasn't with me as he would have only moaned about it being un-British. I hate having to remind him that murderers don't play 'the cricket'.

Dundee Manor is quite large and well decorated and I spotted some nice paintings. One was even by my wife, Troy. There was plenty of information to make a note of though not much in the way of conventional problems.

The game hangs together very well and the solution has plenty of little twists that will keep you on your toes. It's a pity that this isn't a Columbo mystery... then you'd know who did it in advance!

As normal with a Lockerby game the presentation is excellent. The location text is short and to the point, but there's plenty of additional text messages. Taking a quick peek at the PAW database shows a lot of unused memory on the 128K, it's a pity this couldn't have been utilised but, then again, it's still one of Jack's most enjoyable adventures to date.

The Occult Connection (Sam)

Written by David Munden

Published by the Sam Adventure Club

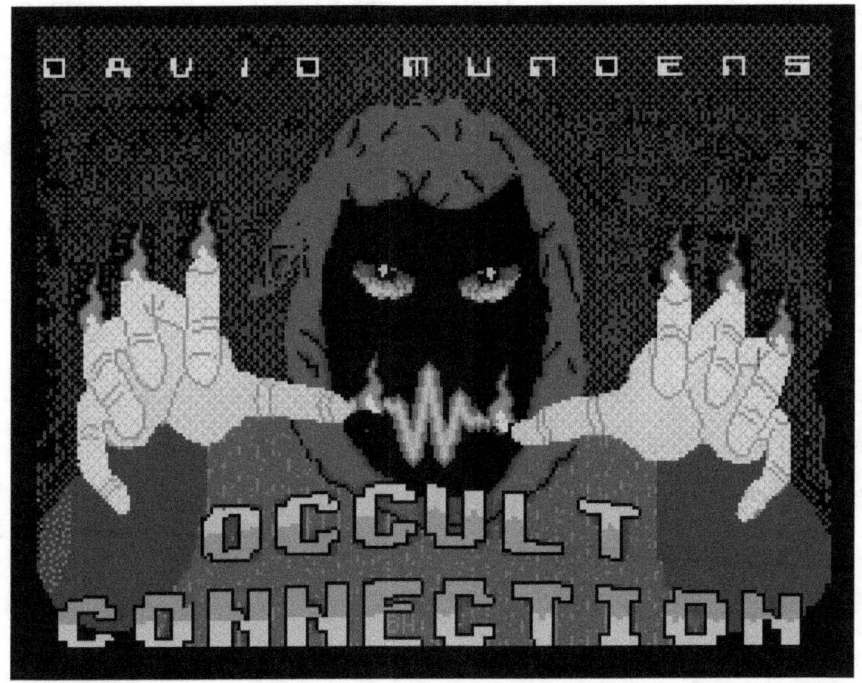

In the spirit of 'Methyhel', you take on the role of a psychic writer in this, the first 'full' SASed (Sam Adventure System) adventure. You have to stop the murders that have been happening in your village... the police think it is the work of a madman who delights in burning people to death, but you know better... it is a demon.

Indeed, your first task is to evade the same fate as the other victims. You have to find some method of protection against the demonic attacks. The book of spells that you discover in your house, which is where you start, points you in the right direction and after going around your home and EXAMINing things (making sure you check UNDER them) you will soon get together the necessary equipment to lead a 'charmed' life.

Once that first task (which earns you about a quarter of the points in the game) is over it's out into your village/town. The portable phone that you find, that you carelessly dropped in the garden, will keep you in touch with various friends who will be able to give you a bit of knowledge of the Occult. Then you'll need to find a way of getting your car going and also a bit of cash.

Gruesome happenings abound, and you should prepare yourself for the sight of more than a few dead bodies... this is definitely not a game for the faint-hearted.

There are a few great problems – including one involving a car alarm and the one in the garage. There are quite a lot of locations that are simply there to take up space, but you need such rooms in a game like this in order to preserve the reality of a town (how often have you found yourself in an adventure town with just one house and a single shop?)

Despite the large number of locations, it's not a huge game and it won't keep you going for months on end... but it will keep you occupied for a good few weeks at least.

On the programming side – Text is nicely highlighted, with different types of messages being in different colours. You can change the font and the palette to suit your TV/monitor and your eyes, though the default colours and set are quite readable.

I did notice one or two little bugs but the author assures me he has now put them right so I won't go into them. At certain points the parser is a bit restrictive – it only accepts inputs along a certain line of thought... sometimes you find yourself thinking up complex inputs for a problem that is solved simply, like I did with the ball of twine.

There are spells, blood and guts aplenty. If you like paranormal adventures then check this one out. I look forward to seeing David's next SAS. As for this one – Well, it's well written, nicely presented, very reasonably priced and a great first-effort at an adventure by the author... check it out!

The Sam Coupe was a graphically-advanced Spectrum clone that appeared late in the life of the 8-bit machines at a time when most people were moving on to either 16-bit computers or videogame consoles. It had very little commercial software produced for it, but it became popular with a small group of adventurers who set up the Sam Coupe Adventure Club and magazine.

Out of the Limelight (Spectrum 48K)

Written by Jonathan Scott & Stephen Boyd

Published by Zenobi Software

Ah! The theatre! The smell of grease-paint! The thrill of treading the boards! Surprisingly, for a game with a theatrical setting, little is seen of the stage or anyone connected to it. Still...

'Out of the Limelight' concerns Sir Ignatius Grimwood, the celebrated thespian, and his attempts to track down the person who attempted to murder his friend, and fellow actor, Obadiah Hardy. Grimwood knows who the attacker was but his only hope in capturing him and bringing him to justice lies in locating the villain's henchman, Jeremiah Plantagenet.

Now Ignatius knows that Jeremiah will probably be found at a certain hotel in Creighton, so he intends to travel there. Ignatius starts the game in the centre of the "city"... a strange place that only consists of three locations – the city centre, an alleyway and a pawnshop. In the alleyway is a young lad by the name of Ralph. Ralph's been separated from his parents, who are also actors, so it's pretty likely that they've gone to Creighton for the season. It's a good idea for Ignatius to make friends with Ralph and get him to tag along with him.

Ignatius will also need Ralph's help regarding the pawnshop. He needs some money, but the only item he's got is his cane and he'll need to figure out some way of getting it back as it needs to be used later. Ralph also helps with a bit of breaking and entering that's needed, if Ignatius is going to get into his lodgings and write the letter that's required to book the room in the hotel that Plantagenet is staying at.

Ignatius has to travel to Creighton by rail. As he can only afford one ticket, a bit of subterfuge is needed to help get Ralph there as well, but his parents will be grateful to Ignatius if he succeeds.

Once at Creighton, Ignatius should report to the hotel. He'll need to do a bit of WAITing to get certain objects and he'll also have to find some way of getting around paying the bill! Of course, he'll have to decide how to deal with Plantagenet when he finds him as well!

'Out of the Limelight' is a 'serious'-ish game. The fact that it's written by two different people gives the game a very off-centre feel – with the humour of Scott failing to blend in amongst the seriousness of Boyd. The game also suffers from the worst screen presentation I've seen for a long time... a possible problem caused by lack of memory?

The game isn't really that big, and I suspect again, that this is due to fact that a lot of the memory has been taken up by character interaction routines. Users of PAW will know that the SAY TO "" type routines eat away at the memory like mad, and they've been used quite extensively here.

The game has its fair share of strange inputs. BEFRIEND RALPH isn't immediately obvious... even if the clue is in the text. CONCEALing an object is rather more straightforward, but you have to RETRIEVE it later – It's a good job these two were on the Zenobi command sheet, together with others like BRUSH, EXTRACT, PRETEND, SILENCE, and REPAIR.

The game is played in PAW 'real-time'. PAUSE stops the clock. You can pass the time typing WAIT, or WAIT HOUR and this comes very useful later when you're waiting for scheduled events.

I didn't really enjoy this game at all. I felt that it was too disjointed. The puzzles were okay but they didn't really hang together very well, and I was more than a little confused by certain plot points and events in the game.

Prison Blues (Spectrum 48K)

Written by Simon Avery

Published by The Guild

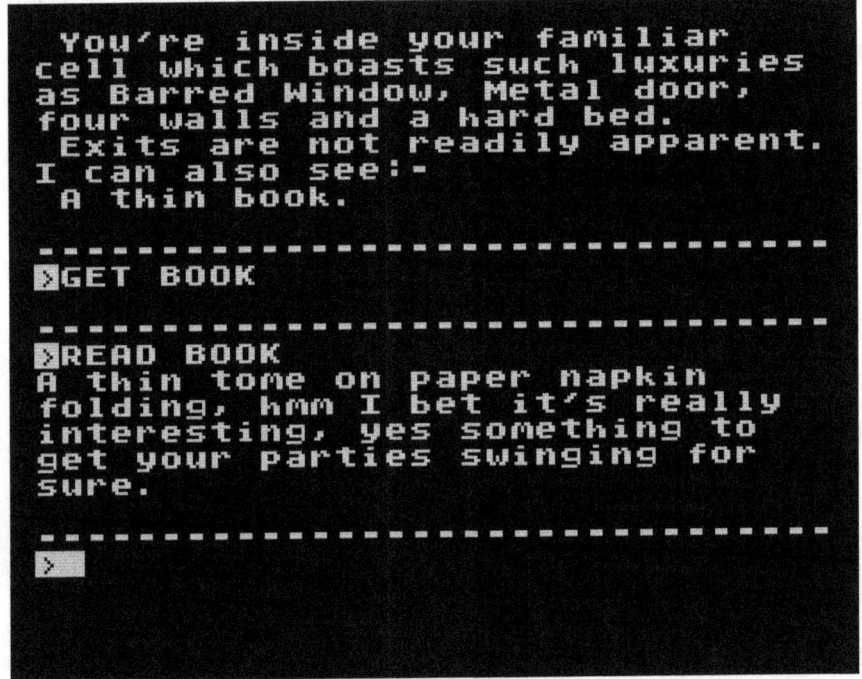

```
   You're inside your familiar
cell which boasts such luxuries
as Barred Window, Metal door,
four walls and a hard bed.
   Exits are not readily apparent.
I can also see:-
  A thin book.

■ ■ ■ ■ ■ ■ ■ ■ ■ ■ ■ ■ ■ ■ ■ ■ ■ ■ ■ ■ ■ ■ ■ ■
▶GET BOOK

■ ■ ■ ■ ■ ■ ■ ■ ■ ■ ■ ■ ■ ■ ■ ■ ■ ■ ■ ■ ■ ■ ■ ■
▶READ BOOK
A thin tome on paper napkin
folding, hmm I bet it's really
interesting, yes something to
get your parties swinging for
sure.

■ ■ ■ ■ ■ ■ ■ ■ ■ ■ ■ ■ ■ ■ ■ ■ ■ ■ ■ ■ ■ ■ ■ ■
▶
```

'Prison Blues' is yet another QUILLed game by Simon Avery. In it, you play a desperate criminal who has plans of escaping from the prison he's currently in. At least I assume that YOU play the criminal, but it does get rather confusing as the location text and messages refer to 'YOU' but the system messages refer to 'I'.

The game starts in your cell. The presentation is really ancient QUILL standard. Everything is white on black, and lines of '-'s separate each response and message. As with 'The

Magician's Apprentice', whenever you discover an object the game merely prints 'I find something!' and you have to REDESCRIBE the location to see what the object actually is.

The cell where you start contains a barred window, a metal door, four walls and a hard bed. EXAM WINDOW and you discover that a metal bar is loose. Pulling the bar removes it from its place in the window. Having a closer look at the bed reveals a book. Inside the book is a credit card which comes in handy to open the door with.

Once you're out of the cell you find yourself in a corridor running north to south. Up to the north is another prisoner's cell. EXAMining his bed produces some strange pink pills. Being the adventurer you are, you will no doubt try to eat them, in which case you'll find that you doze off to sleep and the guards come and take you away.

It's about now that you'll realise there's no RAMSAVE feature. Which will make you scream when you walk into the guard's rest-room by accident and get killed off, yet again.

To relieve all this pent in anger, go and bash the other prisoner, in the cell where you got the pink pills, on the head. If you do that you'll notice that he's wearing the uniform of a 'trustee'. This will come in very handy if you decide to enter the guard's room again.

You'll also find the use of the command INFO helpful. It displays some commands used in the adventure. Looking down the list of possible inputs, one should immediately jump out as being useful. You have some pink sleeping pills and the guard is drinking a cup of coffee... aha... DRUG COFFEE is the command needed, and once you've done that you can nick the guard's keys if you like.

```
 You're inside your familiar
cell which boasts such luxuries
as Barred Window, Metal door,
four walls and a hard bed.
 Exits are not readily apparent.

- - - - - - - - - - - - - - - - - - - - - - - -
>EXAMINE DOOR
There is a small gap on one side

- - - - - - - - - - - - - - - - - - - - - - - -
>EXAMINE GAP
Half way down you can see a
catch.

- - - - - - - - - - - - - - - - - - - - - - - -
>I
I am carrying...
Nothing much.

- - - - - - - - - - - - - - - - - - - - - - - -
>
```

This will enable you to enter the hospital wing of the prison, where you'll come across a bed with a sign above it. The sign reads "The first few moments of life are the most dangerous, and underneath someone has scrawled the words "The last few are a bit dodgy too!" On the bed are some sheets and it's here that my enjoyment of the game was totally ruined.

I had got the sheets and tied them together to make a rope. On returning to my cell I tied the rope to the window. However, I couldn't seem to be able to climb down it, so I untied the rope again. OK so far, but then I typed GET ROPE. 'It's not here'. Pardon? GET ROPE. 'It's not here'. GET SHORT ROPE. GET SHEETS. GET THE ROPE MADE OUT OF SHEETS, GET THE FLIPPIN ROPE. 'It's not here'. Okay, Okay. I typed LOOK and low and behold I was told that 'I can see a short rope'. Argggh!!! It wasn't tied to anything and yet I couldn't get it. And what's more, I appeared to have lost 5% from my score by undoing the rope.

'PRISON BLUES' isn't a bad game. In fact, I was enjoying it up to the rope bit. But it looks very dated, even though it was written in 1991 (and presumably converted to the Spectrum recently), and against the competition – Laurence Creighton's QUILLed games, it just doesn't hold its own. I have a feeling, as Simon's games are so highly regarded on the Amstrad, that it's the cheap and cheerful conversion process that has ruined what might have been an otherwise enjoyable adventure.

Run Bronwyn Run (Spectrum 48K)

Written by Larry Horsfield

Published by FSF Adventures

```
You are in the main room of your
apartment in the castle. It is
sparsely furnished, with just a
table and two chairs, a settee,
and two armchairs that sit
either side of the fireplace. An
archway leads south into your
bedchamber and, opposite the
windows, there is a wooden door.
What now?
>EXAMINE WINDOWS
The windows look out over the
castle courtyard. They are all
closed.

What next?
>OPEN WINDOWS
OK.

What do you want to do next?
>
```

'Run Bronwynn Run' was the first ever 'Megapoints' game at the first ever 'Adventure Probe Convention' and now, at long last, the full version has been made available to the general public.

The adventure is an 'escape' game set in Larry Horsfield's fantasy world that appeared in 'The Axe Of Kolt' and 'Spectre Of Castle Coris'. The game spans a massive three 48K parts and puts you in the high-heeled shoes of Princess Bronwynn. Princess Browynn's parents, The King and Queen of Alizon, plan to marry her off to a middle-aged wally called Prince Timothy. Bronwynn isn't too chuffed about this and decides to do a runner to her cousin Kelson's kingdom of Hecate. There is one tiny little problem... Guards are all over the place to stop her leaving, and even if she does get out there's the fact that Hecate lies many miles away and she'll have to travel THROUGH Karsten to get there... Which just happens to be the kingdom in which Tim, her intended, lives!

Still, Bronwynn doesn't let that bother her and after a quick search round her room (acquiring a change of clothes and a piece of paper that will be of great use to her later) she exits through the window. She walks along the windowsill and leaps across to a nearby stairwell.

The main gate is watched over by guards and so Bronwynn indulges in a little bit of subterfuge. She is no dummy... but what she uses is. Once the coast is clear she ventures out into the city with the basic plan being to find her old Nanny who has a house somewhere near the cathedral.

At first it seems like a hopeless task because she is in a maze of alleyways, but after consulting the piece of paper she found in her room she finds that her progress is greatly assisted by thinking of a clock-face and compass directions.

After several wrong turns and a hectic chase Bronwynn finally gets to her Nanny's house. unfortunately, it seems that she isn't in... but Bronwynn is a girl of many talents and forces an entry. Once inside, though, she finds out that her Nanny's upstairs asleep. She doesn't wake her but makes an escape through the back way of the house. Here she meets up with her horse and enters the second part.

The second and third installments continue in the same vein with more disguises to wear and tasks to do. You even do a bit of matchmaking! Watch out, though, as danger lies ahead, even on the home straight to Hecate!

The game is of the usual FSF Adventures standard and if, like me, you've played all of Larry's other games you'll know that you'll have to EXAMINE and SEARCH things and even SEARCH UNDER things as well.

Perhaps the second and third parts don't seem to have the polish of the first, but I still rate this as an excellent little game... though unfortunately, like all of Larry's other games, I don't recommend it to beginners as it's quite tricky... especially at the beginning.

Sheriff Gunn (Sam)

Written by Mark Turner

Published by Samurai Software

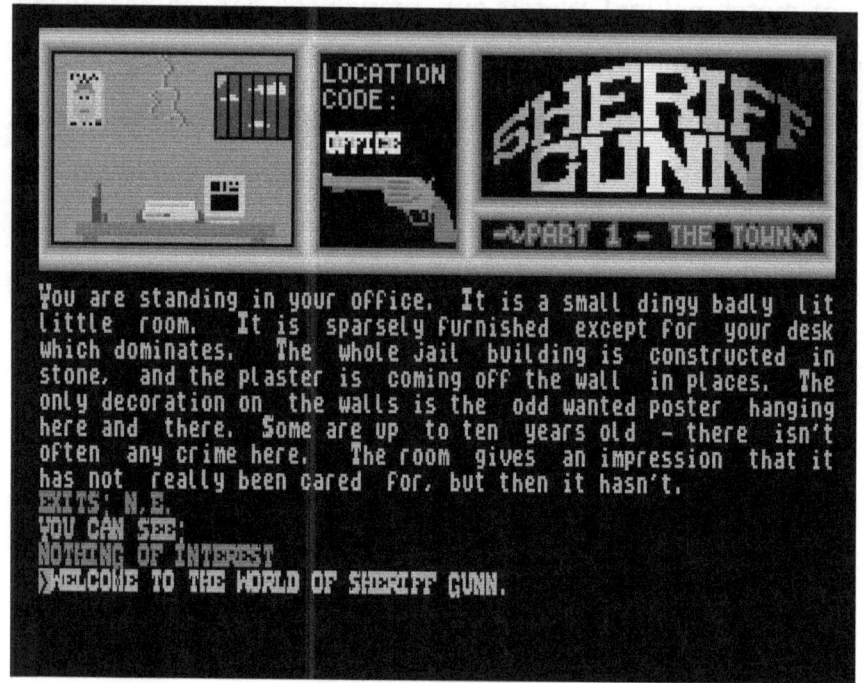

It's time to go back to the year of 1880, and 'The Wild West', for this new Sam Adventure by Mark Turner of Samurai Software. The town of Rock Ridge is plagued by the evil outlaw Poisonous Pete and only one man is good enough for the job. His name is Marshall Axe, a tough, sharpshooting law enforcer. Unfortunately, Marshall Axe has better things to do than save a two-bit town like Rock Ridge, and so the task to get rid of Pete falls instead upon the town sheriff – Sheriff Gunn.

Gunn, although no genius, knows the old proverb 'Safety

in Numbers', so he decides to form a 'posse' to catch Pete. And this is where you come in, playing the part of the good Sheriff.

You start in your office. The top of the screen shows a small, but very colourful, picture of the location while next to that is the location code (more about that later) and the usual game title etc. The graphic in the office location shows a Sam sitting on top of your desk. EXAMINE SAM produces the response – 'Oops, A bit of anachronism slipping in there'. Going north takes you next to your jail. Inside is the town mayor, who had been arrested the night before for being drunk and disorderly. He would like you to let him out. But where is the key?

You have no time to worry about that, for your deputy soon appears and tells you that Pete has robbed the bank! Looks like you'd best get your posse formed rather sharpish!

Getting people to join your posse involves doing good deeds for them. Your deputy, for example, has left his wedding ring in the bedroom of the proprietor of the local saloon. As you can guess, this could be rather embarrassing if his wife found out! Then there's the blacksmith, who wants you to find his children. They went out to play a few hours ago and haven't yet returned.

Rock Ridge is quite large, with over 50 locations to explore, and there are plenty of characters wandering around that will give you tasks to perform.

Once you've got all seven people needed for the posse it's onto part two. This takes place in a separate load, though no password is needed to play it. Due to unforeseen circumstances, you are on your own again and must track down and kill Pete yourself. Watch out for the snakes and other desert perils, though!

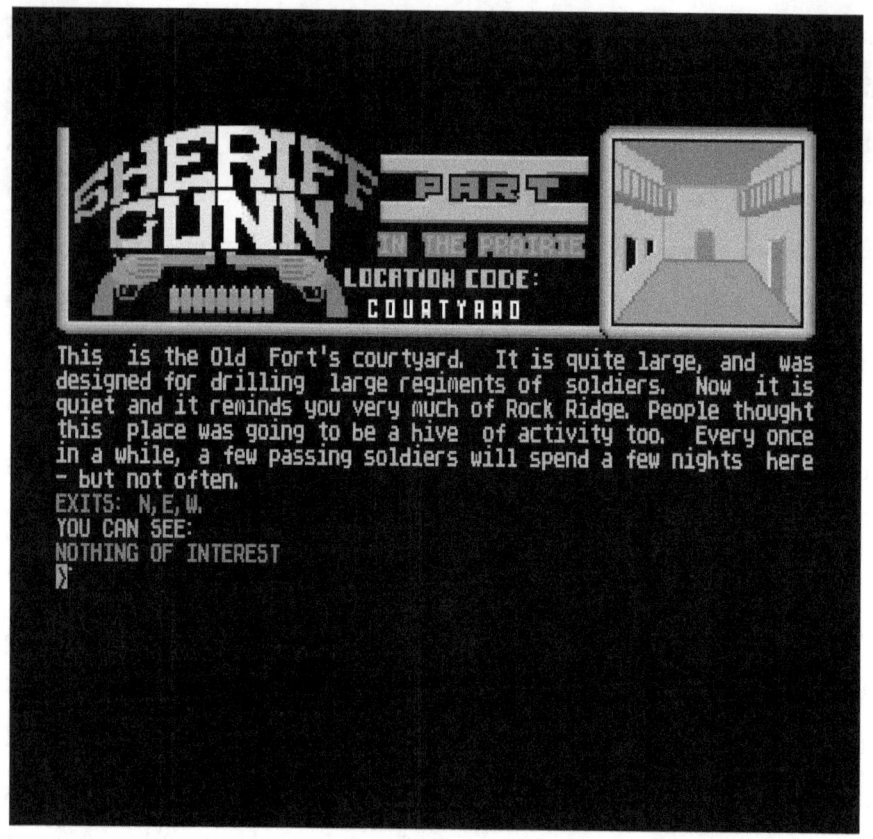

The text is mildly humorous, though sometimes tends to be a bit clumsy in places. The characters are dealt with very well. They will wander in and out of locations, you can talk to them, and they each have a definite personality.

'Sheriff Gunn' is actually mostly written in Sam BASIC –

though it runs so fast that this doesn't make any difference at all. The amount of special commands is huge. You can RUN TO a specific location, to save time, by typing RUN TO (Location Code). You can FIND a character. Ramsave and Ramload are catered for. The usual GET ALL and DROP ALL commands are included. Graphics can be turned on or off. You can change the game colours or the font to a presentation that suits you. The function keys can be used to save you typing in command commands. And for the lazy among you, you can even use the cursor keys as opposed to the normal compass command input.

With okay graphics, 64 column text, 80 locations and over 20 other characters 'Sheriff Gunn' is quite impressive. Seasoned adventurers will make steady progress, as the puzzles aren't that hard, but it makes an excellent beginners introduction to adventuring and will hopefully succeed in getting more Sam owners interested in the genre.

Star Flaws (Spectrum 48K)

Written by Scott Denyer

Published by Delbert the Hamster Software

```
nuke Skyporker stood, well
crouched, in the rather
claustrophobic secret hiding
place. It was scarcely
furnished, apart from a few
crates lying around. nuke was
upset that Yan Polo had not
taken the time to make it a bit
more welcoming.
The only exit was a small hatch
that led up.
::::::::::::::::::::::::::::::::::::::::::::

What should nuke do now?
*EXAMINE HATCH
It's a small hatch, just big
enough to climb up through. On
the other side, it is
camouflaged as a floor tile.

What now, nuke?
**
```

Delbert the Hamster, in case you don't recognise the name, is a fairly new Speccy software company whose previous games include 'Arnold the Adventurer' (for Zenobi) and 'Desmond and Gertrude'. In this latest, text-only release, the action takes place a long time ago, in a galaxy some millions of miles west of the Watford Gap... yes, it's Star Wars spoof time!

You take control of Nuke Skyporker, a young space cadet and must guide him on his mission to rescue the pretty (and extremely bad tempered, from what I've seen) Space Princess.

Your companions, Yan Polo and Tobacco the Cookie (groan) seem to have legged it, so it's up to you to take on the might of the evil Empire (led by the infamous Daft Radar).

The game opens up with a neatly printed title screen and an introduction to the story, printed in typical space style, one letter at a time, and manages to be funny without trying too hard. You start on board your ship, the Millennium Sparrow, and from there, if you manage to pass the first few obstacles, you move into the Deaf Star itself and take on Daft Radar's soldiers. The game takes place in real time. If you walk into a room full of soldiers you have less than a second (well it feels like that anyway) to take some action against them. I don't think that is enough time really, but luckily it's quite easy to "cheat" by pressing a key immediately when you enter a location – this fools PAW into thinking you are typing a move.

The game has the usual memory SAVE/LOAD features and the option of changing the font – which is good as I found the standard one hard to read. On the subject of text, I did feel that maybe it got slightly repetitive at times – mind you, you try thinking up new descriptions for several "corridor" locations. Good use is made of PAW though, and the game is smartly presented with several special FXs throughout. The best bit, for me, was the final conversation between Daft Radar and young Nuke – it is really funny.

Star Flaws is definitely bigger than 'Desmond & Gertrude', although I thought it still lacked a few puzzles. What's there is "hardish" and I guarantee that the use of a sausage is original!

Delbert doesn't lose any marks for packaging. The game comes in a green cassette box (similar to 'Desmond & Gertrude's) that is accompanied by several pages of notes which include pictures of the main characters, a brief plot outline, notes on playing the game and hints on tape loading.

A common moan about 'Desmond & Gertrude' was that it was slightly overpriced but for £1.99 and with the free game on the other side of the tape (entitled 'Raymond Pringle's Quest for the Fabled Jar of Pickled Cabbage') Star Flaws turns out to be a bargain. I know spoofs aren't everybody's cup of tea, but most people will like this as Delbert has an extremely "laid back" style which doesn't force jokes onto you.

Overall, it's not the most complex game ever but it's well presented and definitely fun and in my little world of adventuring, that counts for a lot!

The Taxman Cometh (Spectrum 48K)

Written by Steve Clay

Published by Zenobi Software

Normally when someone fails to pay their taxes they are sent a letter. But when a whole district ignores the hated brown envelopes, the Taxman is unleashed. This time, the district of Tripe-on-Wold has failed to pay their dues and you are the one who must guide the designated revenue officer on his rounds.

A few useful commands can help you. PAID informs you who has paid. EXITS toggles the display of all exits on/off. FONT switches between the available typefaces, while FX turns the sound effects on or off. The way you talk to a character is easy. You simply type the character's name followed by the speech e.g. PHOEBE "EAT SCONE". Then there's all the usual stuff you'd expect in a PAWed game. But what of the actual adventure itself?

The taxman starts on the jetty. A quick type of 'PAID' tells him that he needs to collect money from Halfpint, Lofty, Topper, Odsok, Phoebe and Jeff. That should be an easy task for a Taxman of his calibre. By guiding him around you find that the parser is lacking in a few departments. 'EXAM' isn't accepted as an abbreviation of EXAMINE, but at least 'X' is there as an alternative. What's slightly more annoying is the fact that to read the location description again you have to 'R'edescribe. The more standard 'L'ook won't work.

The above moans were instantly forgotten as I came across several of the initial puzzles. Something is trapped in a toll-box and you have to try and set the thing free, for good deeds earn their rewards in this game. Politeness is also required when dealing with unusual characters like the talking lock who, if you ask nicely, will open the chest that he belongs to, for you.

Pretty soon, like me, you'll come across the first real challenge; a sliding block puzzle. You find some magical steps that are numbered in the wrong order so you are unable to climb them. Elsewhere are some blocks, in separate locations, numbered in exactly the same order. What you have to do is rearrange the blocks, and thus the steps, in the order 1 – 2 – 3 – 4 – 5. Easy? No. The thing is the blocks will only move when you enter certain locations, and each of the locations move different blocks. A lot of logical thought is needed to work out the correct order of visiting the locations.

```
{Near bridge}
An abandoned toll-box stands on
the bank of the river.
A plank bridge stands raised on
the southern side of the river.I
can see a small hut to the west.
I hear a small voice from
somewhere.
Exits: W E S.

       ∞∞∞∞∞∞∞∞∞

{Next}
>LISTEN
I hear a voice "LETMEOUTAERE!!!"

{Next}
>I
I carry:
a pin-striped suit (worn)

{Next}
>
```

After knocking on a few doors you'll come across some of the other characters in the game. Jeff says he can't pay his taxes because his agent can't sell his work. When you see the sample of his work you won't be surprised!

The quest for another tax leads you to an underground dungeon where the non-tax payer challenges you to a game of hide and seek. He even gives you a staff and a spell to help you. Pretty soon you'll find out that this underground sub-section is tough. I got stuck in the storeroom location when I couldn't solve the riddle. Frustration followed as I reset my computer, then instantly reloaded the game – It wasn't beating me. The answer, with hindsight, is remarkably simple – IF you read the question properly!

What's not so easy is the problem involving the trapdoor and the bookshelf. There are no hints for that one – Suffer yourself!!

The game appears to be huge. There are plenty of locked doors, challenges and characters. It's a real hotch-potch of ideas and situations, but one that is held together well by the 'tax collecting' theme. One thing for sure is you won't be finishing it quickly – There's plenty to challenge even the most experienced of adventurers.

Nice short, and to the point, location text and good EXAMINE messages help to make this game even better. An impressive first game and one that you all should find time to have a look at. Maybe it's slightly too hard for beginners, but advanced and intermediate 'bods' will love it. I look forwards to Steve's next title.

Tax Returns (Spectrum 48K)

Written by Steve Clay

Published by Zenobi Software

Many of you will have played Steve Clay's award-winning game (Best 8-Bit Adventure Of 1992), 'The Taxman Cometh', and you'll be pleased, no doubt, to hear that "The Taxman Returneth" in this new adventure.

This time, those who haven't paid are the Devious Debtors of The Diamond Mine – Snow White and the Seven Short Guys. The task is obvious, guide the Taxman around the mine and collect all the outstanding debts.

I started outside the mine... unfortunately I couldn't enter it because there was no light; the Taxman seemed a bit of a coward. Luckily nearby was a Light Generation Tower. Getting it to do its bit was a simple matter, all I had to do was solve a small floor puzzle... turn all the squares in a 3*3 grid from red to green.

Movement around the mine was achieved using a voice-activated cart. I chose to visit the debtor known as Blotto first. Blotto is always under the influence and it was quite easy to recognise his home by the empty beer barrel outside. In fact, that proved very helpful in getting in and parting Blotto from his taxes. One down and seven to go.

I went to the local nightclub next. Potboy runs this establishment and he promised to pay his debt if I managed to arrange the barrels in his cellars correctly. This took a bit of thought, as it was another simple 'sliding-block' type puzzle, but I soon had the task completed and crossed another debtor off my list.

The dunce of the diamond mine, Nomarks, parted with his cash quite easily and managed to cause a lot of laughs in the process. I took advantage of him slightly by using one of the objects he gave me before giving it back to him.

That object helped me to get in and see Gadget, a mad inventor if ever I saw one. I barely had time to scribble down a clue that I found before he grabbed me and enrolled me in an experiment. Unfortunately, it went wrong... but I managed to return to the lab by using my brain and being very careful in the order I did things. Gadget made it up to me with an object that helped with my next client's puzzle.

That client was Banker... a person so 'tight' that his nickname was 'Squeaky'. He had his money well hidden away and it was quite hard to get at... I really needed an extra pair of hands but had to make do with a bit of cunning and inventiveness.

After Banker I tracked down Snow White. A wimpy Prince, suffering from piles, opened the door. It seemed that Snow White had been placed in a trap and I had to get her out before she could pay up. Elementary maths is needed to solve some equations that tell you how to deal with the alarms.

Snow White gave me the password I needed to get in to Trapper the fabled trap-builder's lair. He had his loot protected by a devious puzzle that involved a riddle. It kept me thinking for quite a while until I realised that I was looking for a container... after that it was plain sailing.

Last, but not least, was Trapper's apprentice Parser. He had devised a nice little puzzle that needed quite a bit of thought. Remembering proverbs and nursery rhymes came in handy and I soon had my last lot of dosh.

Steve's sense of humour is evident throughout the game... though he writes with a very light touch and never overdoes the jokes. When something is really obvious he wastes no time in telling you... at one point you come across a 'coin-sized slot' and later you find a 'slot-sized coin'; no prizes for guessing what to do here.

What I loved about 'Tax Returns' was that the puzzles

were so decidedly different... it's nice to do some 'Crystal Maze'-style puzzles instead of the usual light lamp/go north/throw water at vampire type of thing. Some aren't overly difficult, but then I'm looking at them with the benefit of hindsight... puzzles always seemed to have been easier once you've worked out the answer.

'Tax Returns' is a great adventure, even more entertaining than 'Taxman Cometh', and I got a real sense of satisfaction when I completed it. If you enjoyed 'The Taxman Cometh' get this game. If you didn't then get it anyway as I can't see anyone not really having fun with this one. Put it on your adventure shopping list at once.

A regular contributor to the pages of 'Adventure Probe' and 'From Beyond', Steve Clay wrote a series of three adventure games about his Taxman character, all of which were released by Zenobi Software. Combining traditional adventure puzzles with logic problems, they're great examples of homegrown adventures from the period.

There is a Bomb under Parliament (Spectrum 48K)

Written by Laurence Creighton

Published by Zenobi Software

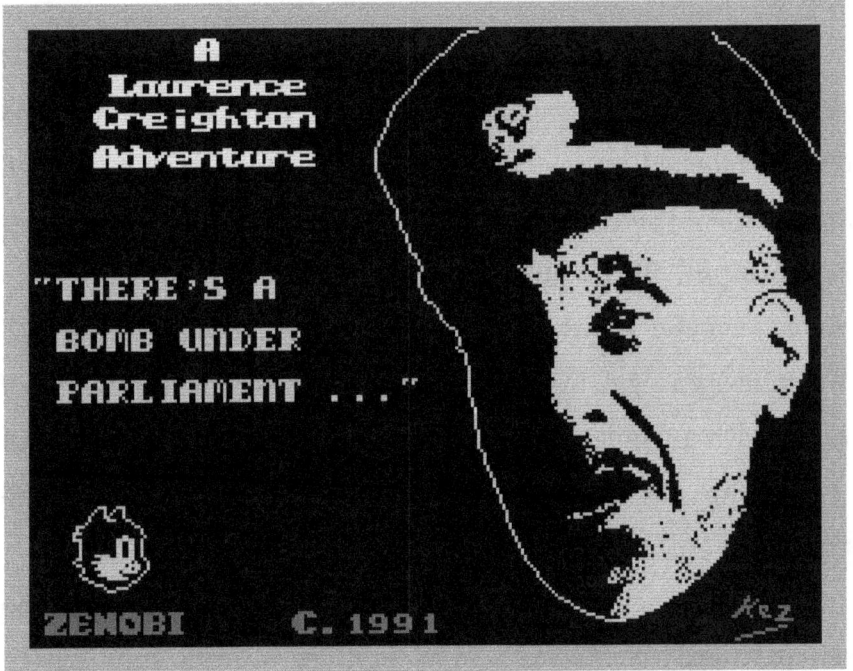

In 'There's a Bomb Under Parliament...' you're a government agent who's received a call that tells you that a bomb has been placed under the parliament building... if you warn anybody, the person who placed it there will explode it. Your only hope is to find the bomb and defuse it. Can you save London? Do you want to?

Rather than search the sewers under Westminster, you've decided to follow up a report that came in a few days ago from a farmer who said he'd noticed strange activity near his hills. The farmer's name is W.Heat and the best way to start is by paying him a visit. He reveals a little more information and tells you that a helicopter came the other day and took all the people from the hill away and since then the strange noises he heard have stopped.

Off you go and investigate. You need to SEARCH everything to find several useful objects. A cave in the hill has its entrance blocked by a steel door which, when you get it open, will probably yield a nasty surprise for you. There's a rather obscure input, PUSH ROCK, needed to find an object nearby and I can't really see what is meant to point you to this.

Once you get inside the cave you discover a network of tunnels with a whole host of offices and workshops inside. A lot of rooms are dark, so you'll need a battery for the torch the farmer gave you if you want to explore them in safety.

There's a few sudden death situations, the booby-trap one was particularly unexpected... I think more warning should have been given here. You have to make sure your carrying certain objects at certain times or you may find yourself stuck in a certain place.

Overall, 'Bomb' is nothing really that special but it does contain quite a lot of puzzles that will keep most players busy. I wouldn't recommend it as a good starting game for beginners, though.

The Treasure of Santa Maria (Spectrum 48K)

Written by Laurence Creighton

Published by Zenobi Software

You've decided to take this year's holiday in Cornwall, and have managed to get hold of a nice little holiday cottage that just needs the deposit and rent paid on it before you can move in. You did think that all you'll be doing on this holiday is resting and eating clotted-cream teas, but when you hear of the treasure of the Santa Maria you decide that you're going to try and find it...

And that's basically how the plot goes of this 48K adventure that was programmed using the Quill. The first set of locations are set in and around the small, unnamed, village that you're holidaying in. One of your initial tasks is to pay the estate agent the necessary money for the cottage... this seems to be a bit of a problem at first – You've got no money on you. Searching the jeans that you're wearing, more than once, will produce a way to get cash, though you'll need to be patient and WAIT around a bit before you can obtain the necessary dosh.

Just when you think you've got access to the cottage you are stopped, not only by a growling dog outside the house, but by the fact that the key that you've got doesn't quite fit. Again, SEARCHing carefully holds the answer to one of the puzzles... what you'll find will get the attention of someone who can help you.

A strange smell can be detected outside and inside the cottage. It doesn't take much to realise that it's the smell of gas, so you should remember all those adverts that used to be on TV if you don't want to die.

The cottage holds a lot of objects... finding them requires more SEARCHing, moving, and careful use of objects already found. There's quite a lot of stuff to locate, but you have to watch out that you don't spend too much time here initially as there is a timed event that you need to get to.

A bus-stop lies across a busy road and you must watch your step as you walk across. Random elements come into play here, so you need to ramsave your position, using RS, before crossing just to make sure that you don't get flattened by a passing juggernaut. Once at the bus-stop you may manage to get a bus pass with which you can get to the jetty.

At the jetty lots of seamen seem eager for your trade. An object found earlier will help you to CHOOSE the right person. Then they'll take you out to where you think the sunken wreck is... It's here that most of the adventure takes place.

You need to DIVE and investigate the wreck. Your sailor pal will often help you out if you ask him. You need to make sure that you SURFACE before you run out of air.

To reach the treasure requires good use of objects found earlier. I particularly liked the octopus problem and opening the chest near the end.

'Treasure' is a decent game, filled with puzzles that you should enjoy providing you can get past the initial, first few hurdles. Recommended for the intermediate gamer.

UK-born Laurence Creighton moved to Cape Town, South Africa when he was young. A devotee of Gilsoft's Quill adventure writing system, he penned over twenty adventures for the Spectrum.

T'was a Time of Dread (Spectrum 48K)

Written by Clive Wilson

Published by Zenobi Software

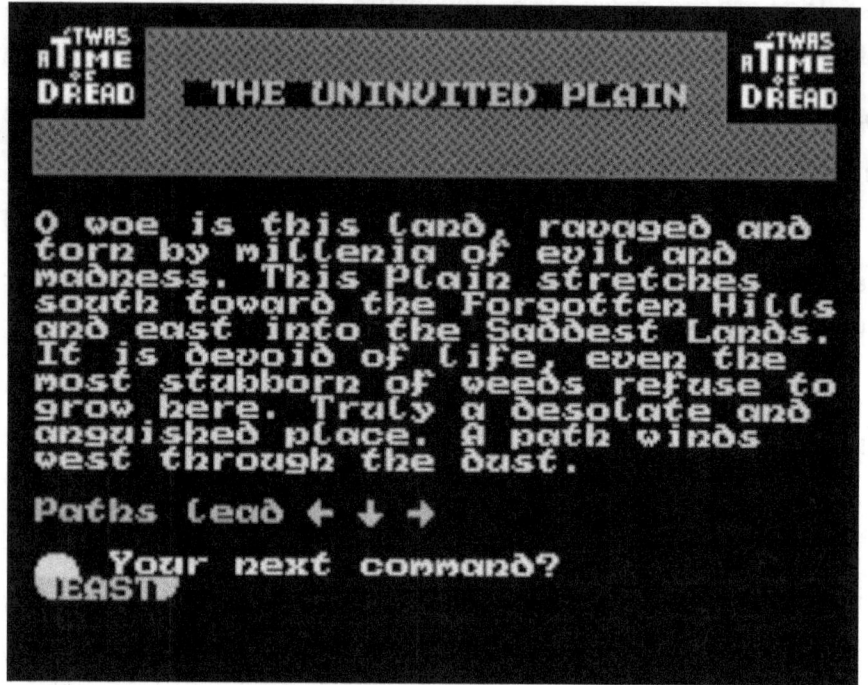

'T'was a Time of Dread' is the concluding part of the 'Darkest Road Trilogy', and I don't think that fans of Clive's earlier titles will be disappointed by this game at all.

It's many a long year (three thousand really, if you want to be pedantic!) since the Mysterious Stranger last set foot in these lands. But now, when the once beautiful country has been destroyed, he returns.

He visits you, for you are a descendant of the 'Singer of the Song', and tells you the tales of 'The Black Wanderer' and his evil creation the 'Unborn One'. He tells you that he created another being, a being that has mutated over the many years into many. That being called its number the Legion.

Only you, and the power of the Silent Song, can combat this evil menace and banish it from the land.

You start in the 'saddest lands' whose description lies beneath a garish band of colour. A quick wander around will see your untimely demise – well it will if like me you just walk around without reading the location text! There are plenty of places to visit; woods, marshes, plains and even a small town can be explored.

At one point in the game you'll find an object that will give you some cryptic clues. These will appear in the space above the location description – I had wondered what it was for!

The game is full of lots of puzzles. They seem to be wide ranging in difficulty, giving the player plenty of chance to warm up before they come up to something really difficult. I think this game is a lot more challenging overall than the rest of the trilogy, it just starts a lot easier.

The text is generally well done and the responses are a lot better than in Clive's earlier games. I feel that humour is nice to see in a game, but I felt that it was a little out of place at times in this adventure. It tended to break the flow of the rest of the, more serious text. I much preferred Clive's long, descriptive passages.

The usual Clive special FXs appear as well, and the layout of the screen will be instantly recognisable to fans of the series.

One thing that is apparent is that Clive appears to have been taking note of reviews of his earlier titles. Not only has he cut down the number of sudden deaths, but he's also stopped including the problems that require things to be examined CLOSELY or pushed HARD. Instead he's made the puzzles more original and three-dimensional. It's good to see Clive listening to the people who play his games (something I wish more adventure writers would do). He certainly deserves the large following that he now has.

To sum up the game, I think that it's much better than the previous games in the trilogy ('The Darkest Road' and 'The Unborn One') and it should while away several nights.

Clive Wilson collaborated with Les Hogarth on several commercially released icon-driven adventures. His solo titles, produced using the PAW and released by Zenobi, included a sequel to his Mastertronic hit, Kobyashi Naru (Kobyashi Ag'Kwo) as well as The Darkest Road trilogy.

The Violator of Voodoo (Spectrum 48K)

Written by The Traveller in Black (Ian S. Brown)

Published by Zenobi Software

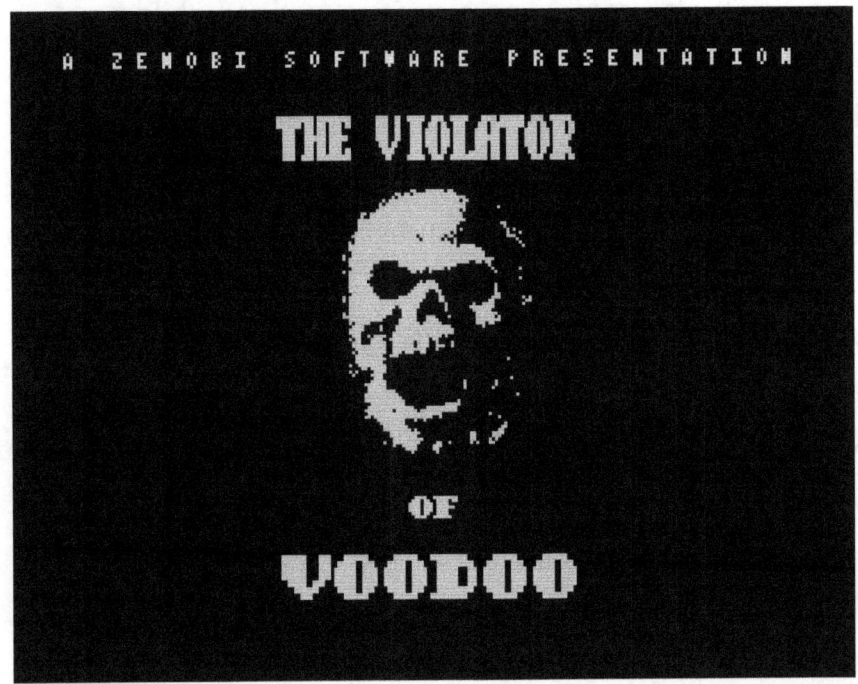

'Violator of Voodoo' is the follow up to the highly acclaimed, and award winning, 'Phoenix'. The great temporal struggle between the evil might of the Abomination and Chronos's Time Crusaders continues. The island of Santo Barbaro in the Caribbean has been overrun by the demons of the Primal Darkness. Chronos has no choice but to send two of his crusaders to fight the evil menace this time – Kane of The Cloudlands and yourself, Phoenix.

You start on the island, inhabited by followers of that

often-misunderstood religion – Voodoo. In the distance you can hear the islanders, under the influence of the Abomination, chanting in an unknown tongue. The island is rather vast and there's a few blocked locations due to monsters and zombies.

You'll also come across various tortured children. In a small gully there's a headless body, while tied to a boulder on the edge of a cliff is another demented child. Something tells me that helping them isn't going to be easy.

It's a good idea if you make a good map of the island, as it is large and you need to be able to get from one place to another quite easily. Eventually you should come across the two religious leaders of the island. The first, The Houn'gan (Priest) doesn't seem to be able to help you too much, due to the minor fact that he's dead. The Mambo (Priestess) is more use and is the key character in the game.

The Mambo will guide your actions on the island. She will tell you what you need to do next and what objects to bring her. Talking of objects, there are plenty of them about. They range from the ordinary type (bowl, sledgehammer etc.) to objects associated with Voodoo. Things like assons (a rattle) and assens (an iron rod on a plate). Watch out, though, many objects are breakable so don't drop them willy-nilly.

Completing 'The Violator of Voodoo' will definitely challenge you, as Phoenix. Don't expect too much help from Kane, your fellow Time Crusader; when you find him he'll be in a rather bad way. He also asks you to do something unusual to him, although if you remember the end of the last game and also the very nature of a Crusader's life, it isn't really too unexpected.

```
Beside you, partially covered
with kelp and seaweed, is a
small sailing boat that is no
longer seaworthy due to the
powerful hurricane that swept
this region last month. The
beach is to the west or
north-east.
~~~~~~~~~~~~~~~~~~~~~~~~~~~~~~~~
What should you do now?
>NE
Further along the beach, a
multi-limbed horror from the
Primal Darkness notices your
advance and decides to quickly
leave, carrying a large
blood-covered object under one
of its arms.



    Press any key to continue.
```

The island is wonderfully described. The author has really taken time on the game and has painted a realistic picture. There are many references to the Voodoo religion (the common terms of which, are described on the information sheet that comes with the game).

The presentation has gone up several notches since 'Phoenix'. There are none of the slap-dash, badly formatted messages this time round. The screen layout is clear, with the location descriptions at the top split from the rest of the text by a line of UDGs. The parser is excellent on the whole, although in a few cases it maybe asks you to be a bit too specific.

'The Violator of Voodoo' is an excellent game which should prove a challenge for the whole spectrum of adventure players. The pace is leisurely and beginners won't find themselves rushed by the whole thing, while the more advanced adventurer should make good progress but still find themselves scratching their heads on several occasions.

After the hype, I was disappointed with 'Phoenix' when I played it. 'Violator', however, is everything that people told me 'Phoenix' was, and more. Buy it.

Ian S. Brown wrote the four games in the 'Phoenix' series under the pseudonym 'The Traveller in Black' as they were completely different in tone and style to his earlier, humorous adventures 'Bog of Brit' and 'The Menagerie'

The Weaver of Her Dreams (Spectrum 48K)

Written by Mike White

Published by 8th Day / GI Games / Zenobi Software

I found myself in a dimly lit library. Several facts presented themselves immediately – Firstly, I was being referred to as a 'she'. I could live with that. What I found unbearable, however, was the glare from the white paper/black text presentation method. Oh well, at least my current score and number of turns left (to what, I wondered?) was nicely visible at the top of the screen.

Glancing round the library saw the discovery of certain pieces of furniture. A locked cabinet appeared to contain a book.

While a mysterious, and small, table housed a misspelt drawer. The 'draw', when searched, revealed some documents and a further examination produced a key which, I found, would unlock the cabinet.

```
SCORE:  0 / 250    Turns:+ 997
She was beside a small table in
a dimly lit library. A large,
glass fronted bookshelf
dominated the room. A cabinet
was on the east wall, a small
door led south. A raging wind
that howled about the room
seemed to bring the night in
closer.
> EXAMINE TABLE
The desk was made of finely
polished Oak. A draw was closed.
> OPEN DRAWER
This was done.
> LOOK IN DRAWER
The draw was full of old
documents.

> GET DOCUMENTS>
```

I opened the book and instantly found myself entwined in the story. It was as though I was part of the tale, as though...

I found myself on the base of a small rise overlooking an encamped army. An old man stood next to me and told me that my quest was to destroy the evil sorcerer in the dark tower above me. Although my first thought was, "What again?!", I proceeded up the mountain track. I had to, for the old man had given me a magical 'kick in the butt'.

On the top of the rise I took a few seconds rest to check my inventory. I appeared to have a wooden staff with me and I was clad in a cloak and hood. On examining the staff, I found that it lit the surrounding area with a bright blue glow.

Having checked my possessions I proceeded south, towards the castle, only to find that burning flames erupted around me and I was dead. Luckily, I had RAMSAVED earlier and I returned to the very spot that I had died in my first attempt. This time I frantically waved the staff in a vain effort to disperse the flames – and it worked!

Moving further onwards, I came to the front of the tower itself. It was massive and its form might have filled me with dread if it wasn't for its huge 'chimney'. Without even pausing for a RAMSAVE, I was becoming bolder by the second, I entered the tower.

In the tower were several exits, UP, EAST, SOUTH and DOWN. By going UP the stairs I appeared to have set off a trap for a huge fireball rolled down towards me. The way DOWN was no better, for a huge fist tore up from the ground and I was attacked by a 'Magmaron'. Going SOUTH seemed the only thing to do, and yet I merely found an empty room. However, a careful examination yielded a spell and by retracing my steps I found yet another piece of magic. These spells, CRIZP and HYDRO, helped me progress past the hazards and further into the adventure.

Soon I was finding spells left, right and centre. The good thing about them was that they could be used several times. I travelled through fire-ridden furnaces, up 'chimneys' and met all sorts of magical creatures. Creatures like the talking door, Earth Ward, and Wraith. Conventional puzzles seemed thin on the ground – The whole thing seemed more magic orientated.

On several occasions I cursed the parser and the, frankly silly, screen mode used, but I seemed to be enjoying myself. Now if I can only get through this dratted door....

This PAWed game was originally written and published by 8th Day software, but it's now available as a 'GI-Game' via Zenobi. If you're one of those people who scream at the mere sight of a spelling mistake or made-up word then maybe you'd best give this one a miss. This game may be light on traditional puzzles but it's a challenging adventure that was well worth bringing out of the archives and re-releasing.

Other Adventure Games...

Jack Lockerby / River Software

One of the most prolific authors on the ZX Spectrum and indeed the wider adventure scene, Jack Lockerby (working together with his son-in-law, Roger Betts on many titles) authored thirty-five adventures in eight years. Initially self-publishing titles through his River Software label, Jack's back catalogue and new titles went on to be published by Zenobi Software.

The Domes of Sha

The planet Olaxas once thrived, but that was before The War. Now the planet's only inhabitants are the Sha tribe. They know that their planet is dying, but they don't know why, for all the ancient knowledge has been forgotten. You must brave the perils and gather enough strength to leave the valley and discover how to save your people.

'Domes of Sha' is an entertaining game, mainly due to the inclusion of one of my favourite adventuring companions... Grunt! With his help you must journey out of the valley, down tunnels and solve a whole host of devious Lockerby problems and puzzles. A great PAWed game.

The Bounty Hunter

A masterpiece of PAW programming, you are the bounty hunter of the title and you must seek out the viral lifeforms, Viroids, that have escaped onto a planet which consists of over 1,500 locations. Your handy teleportation device allows you to get from one point to another quickly and a simple blast of your pulsar destroys the Viroids. Actually getting to them is far from easy as Jack has placed a whole host of mind-bending puzzles in the way. One of Jack Lockerby's best games.

Into the Mystic

In this one you take the role of a mug who's daft enough to put their life on the line. Your task is to locate where all the magic is going. This seems to be pretty important, or at least that's what Merlin said when he 'volunteered' you for the job. Although not believing him for one moment you decide to have a stab at it – you've got nothing better to do; there's no TV to watch. In fact, without magic your days will be rather dull. So, after bunging on your smock and sandals, off you go.

The whole quest thing doesn't start too well as pretty soon you run into a band of horibble orcs. Luckily, a nifty bit of running enables you to escape their grasp and you watch as they camp out for the night. A few hours of shut eye later, you awake and stare at the sleeping enemies. How are you going to get past them?

The game is the usual puzzle-filled, smartly presented

and polished River adventure that we've come to expect from author Jack Lockerby and includes several of his trademark mazes. There are some unique items to be found, like the magic wand that when waved turns into a stick and the cloak that turns inside out to form a monk's habit.

The Miser

'The Miser' is Jack's version of the Dickens' tale 'A Christmas Carol'. You play the miserly Scrooge and have a limited time to redeem yourself and make up for all your sins. The game is quite difficult and features a great way of travelling between the past, the present and the future.

Treasure Island

Jack's translation of Robert L. Stevenson's book is one of his best adventures. The first part proceeds at rather a hectic pace and things don't get any slower. You guide the young Jim Hawkins around and must succeed in outwitting the pirates and Long John Silver. A great game that benefits from the extra size allowed by having two parts. Pity about the rather annoying first part maze!

Other Games by Jack Lockerby

'The Enchanted Cottage': Your aim is to become a sorcerer. To do this you must pass three tests set by your superiors and solve the secret of the Enchanted Cottage and the Green Door.

'Match Maker': In 'Match Maker' you have to get the Prince and Princess to the church on time. The Prince must have the wedding ring, the Princess must have her bridal gown and bouquet and you must also get a pageboy dressed in a sailor suit.

'The Cup': A rather strange game! A tall story suddenly comes to life and you find yourself as the major player.

'Jack and the Beanstalk': Jack's adaptation of the classic fairy-tale. You'll need all your wits about you if you're to defeat the giant.

'The Challenge': Battle for the leadership of your tribe by completing tasks and quests.

'The Hammer of Grimmold': There are two versions of this game; the original written using The Quill and an updated version produced with the PAW. The fabled hammer has been stolen by Valk, an evil magician and your task is... yes, you've guess it, to get the hammer back. Why can't WE play the evil magician for a change and have to steal the thing?

'Mutant': 'Mutant' takes place on an island that has been used as the site for bomb testing in the past. Now, though, it has been re-inhabited. However, people have seen a strange monster in the mountains and it is your job to track it down, find out what it is, and destroy it. The game features some nice atmospheric text but I definitely wouldn't recommend it for younger players as it can be a bit gory.

'Lifeboat' & 'Davy Jones' Locker': Two connected adventures as 'Davy Jones' Locker' carries on where 'Lifeboat' left off. Both are very strange games but with lots of ingenious puzzles and great leaps of imagination. Both start normally enough, the ship you were travelling on has been destroyed and you and your companions start in the lifeboat. In 'Lifeboat' you eventually move on to an island where you need all your knowledge of nursery rhymes to proceed. Whilst in 'Davy Jones' Locker' you get rescued by a ship... and then strange events start to happen that ultimately lead to a journey down into the depths of the sea.

'The Jade Necklace': You take on the role of Philip Marlowe, private detective and your job is to locate and retrieve a stolen necklace. A great game but it's let down by a very poor parser that doesn't allow much leeway in the commands required to get the job done.

'Realm of Darkness' / 'Witch Hunt': 'Realm of Darkness' sees you on yet another quest to recover some stolen objects and in 'Witch Hunt' you meet a Witch and start on a very weird journey.

John Wilson / Zenobi Software

The godfather of homegrown ZX Spectrum adventures, John Wilson, also known by his character The Balrog, was the mastermind behind the colossal Zenobi Software. Rightly taking great pride in running Zenobi as a commercial operation (with all the overheads this entailed), his company initially started out publishing John's own games before expanding to release titles by other authors. Many adventure games initially released on other homegrown labels eventually made it into John's catalogue, with his reputation for service & quality making Zenobi the best-known and most popular destination for Spectrum adventurers.

An Everyday Tale of a Seeker of Gold

Written in a tongue-in-cheek style reminiscent of Fergus McNeill, this Hobbit-spoof surprised everyone by including both humour and interesting puzzles. Your task is simply to guide reluctant-adventurer Bulbo on his quest for the treasure of the dragon Smog.

You start in your burrow, a rope and chest besides you and some cakes in the over. Once out of the famous green door (don't try the window!) it's into the familiar world of Hobbit spoofs. You'll encounter the Trolls who decided against eating

Bulbo and go down the Golden Dragon for a cat curry instead; because the last time they had halfling they got indigestion. There is Grand Alf and the Dwarves, and also the sneaky little bulbous eyes of the Murky Wood. An enjoyable romp.

Bulbo and the Lizard King

As a Your Sinclair covertape adventure, 'Bulbo and the Lizard King' prompted an avalanche of mail to Mike Gerrard (the then YS adventure columnist) for help. 'Bulbo' is a game I remember fondly and excellent for beginners. With a choice of travelling companions (choose well for you'll need their skills to solve certain problems) there's plenty of character interaction. After donkey throwing, lake crossing, talking to witches, fighting bears, climbing mountains and listening to mice, you'll be set to vanquish Stratos, the evil Lizard King from the land.

Fuddo and Slam

Bulbo returned from his quests laden down with gold only to lose it all in the sport of 'boggling'. He even lost the fabled magic ring as well to a strange guy called Tinny Convant. He slunk into his burrow and became a recluse., refusing to talk to anyone. Many years after (and this is where the story really starts) his nephew Fuddo decided that he would go and look for Bulbo. And so, with his trusty (well, almost) companion Slam he set out on a journey of a lifetime. With dragons, orcs and even an alien mothership in your way, it won't be an easy quest.

From Out of A Dark Night Sky

This game was a slight departure from John Wilson's normal adventures in that it was both serious and sci-fi themed. 'Dark Night' is a challenging, enjoyable game in which you have to dispose of the pods of the alien civilization that's intent on destroying the earth. Puzzles are logical and well thought out, with only the occasional leaps into a sort of dream-sequence slightly spoiling the atmosphere.

The Secret of Little Hodcome

An average game with quite good problems but lacking John Wilson's usual humour. The game takes place in a mysterious village and your first task is to get into the little cottage that you've just bought. Of course, it would have been a whole lot easier if the estate agent had turned up with the front door key! After entering the house you move further afield into your new neighbourhood and must discover the secret of Little Hodcome and how to defeat the evil that has smothered the land.

The Balrog and the Cat

This game is probably John Wilson's best. It's bursting with humour and puzzles and is a good beginner's introduction to the Balrog's games as it's slightly easier than the previously - mentioned titles. Your task is to help a poor cat that's the pet to that well-known magician The Mighty Wassock. There are plenty of funny creatures to meet – from cats to cockroaches.

There are also the usual Balrog characters like Fuddo, Slam and Bulbo putting in appearances. Great fun.

Behind Closed Doors – The Saga

A trilogy of toilet-based adventures (later expanded with a fourth game). Set inside, outside and around the Balrog's bog, they combine subtle (and not so subtle) humour with a huge amount of puzzles for single location adventures. Believe me, if you want to finish these games you'll have to examine, prod and prise a few things that you don't normally touch in a toilet (or anywhere else for that matter). Legendary Spectrum adventure games that are well worth checking out.

Retarded Creatures and Caverns

Well praised in the hallowed pages of Spectrum magazine Your Sinclair, gaining the 'YS Megagame' award from Mike Gerrard, this is one of John's most difficult adventures. You play as a friend of Bulbo, Algernon, who has gone (in Bulbo's place) to Castle Toidi to take part in an adventure. Contains the usual Wilson humour but one for experienced gamers only. I struggled for ages on the first puzzle!

Jon Lemmon / Compass Software

Publishing his games through his Compass Software label, Jon Lemmon quickly built up a reputation for clever and original adventure games. His titles often included neat programming routines to add sound and visual effects. Some of his games even included arcade elements!

Project X: The Microman / The 'O' Zone

These games were both co-written by Tim Kemp (who went on to run his own successful Spectrum adventure fanzine, From Beyond, and also took on the mantel of Your Sinclair adventure columnist after the departure of Mike Gerrard). Even as early Quill games, released back in 1984, they still hold up today.

The first game concerns Professor Neil Richards, the character you play, who has been exposed to mysterious X-Gamma radiation which has caused him to shrink. As you can probably guess the game involves a fair few encounters with what would normally (at full size) give you no problems, and where things like getting out of a car prove challenging. Your objective is to get to your friend's laboratory where you can return to normal.

That's where the second game begins. You now play

Agent 37 and must find out what has happened to the professor.

Demon from the Darkside / The Golden Mask / The Devil's Hand

Together these games form the classic 'Demon from the Darkside' trilogy and again they are Quilled. Mind you, as Jon Lemmon has always been just that little bit ahead of everyone else with regards to tweaking around with the various adventure systems, you could easily forget how old they actually are.

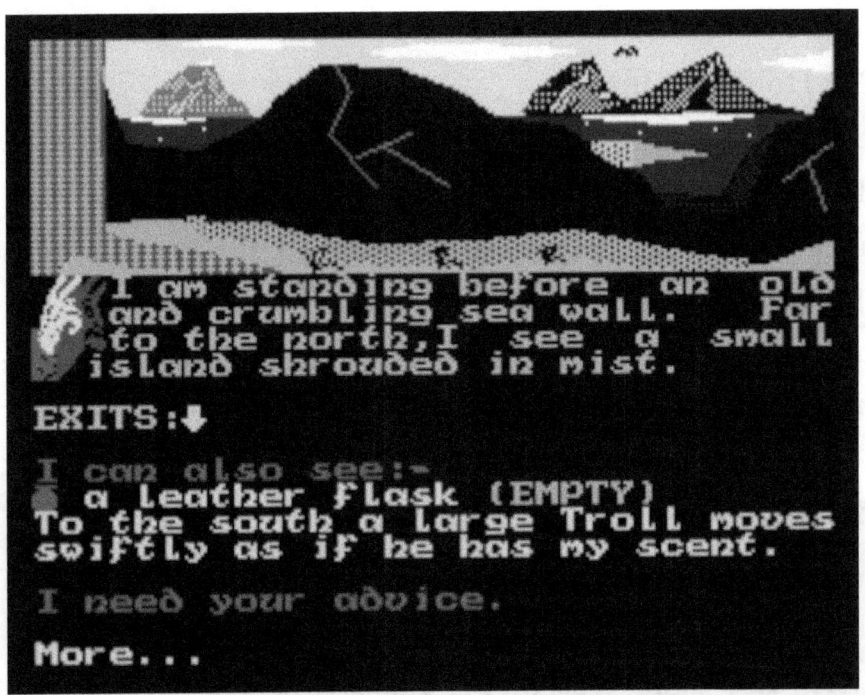

The presentation is very good with decent graphics and lots of little features like Jon's famous compass symbols for exit directions. Each game gets successively harder and together they form a trilogy that should be on the shelves of every adventure. A piece of Spectrum adventure history?

Shadows of the Past

This game is more of a re-write, using the PAW, of 'The Demon from the Darkside' rather than a completely new game. There's still a hell of a lot that's new, though. It's fiendishly difficult as well, with a very hectic start that might easily put many adventurers off it, so maybe you'd best get some practice with the earlier games first.

The Hobble Hunter

A humourous PAWed game that attempts to send up 'The Hobbit'. Thankfully, it does it in an original and moderately successful way with plenty of interesting puzzles to solve. Some of the problems seem a little illogical and lack the usual Compass Software shine however, the game is very well programmed with a heck of a lot going on around you.

The Micro-Mutant

Professor Neil Richard's exploits continue in this PAWed game which features Jon's PIE system (Player Arcade EXTERNS). In this case, the PIE game is a simple one which you must use to boost up your energy in order to mutate. You've now shrunk to the size of an ant, you see, but you can change size if you've collected enough energy. Text purists should take solace in the fact that there is a cheat mode to bypass the PIE game, even if it is quite simple to play. Other fun PAW tweaks in this adventure include a rather good screen shaking effect and lots of sound and other visual effects.

Intruder Alert / Invaders from Planet X

'Intruder Alert' was Jon's first game written using the PAW – not that you'd guess it as it's features all the usual FXs and tweaks that we've come to expect from a Compass game. In this adventure you take on the role of Captain Garth Conrad and you must find what has happened to the science team on the mysterious Planet X. The story continues in 'Invaders from Planet X' where the planet is heading on a collision course with Earth. It's up to you to stop it and also deal with several nasty aliens. There's another PIE game in this one, but it doesn't come until right at the end so don't be put off.

Larry Horsfield / FSF Adventures

Releasing titles on his FSF Adventures label, Larry had a reputation for producing quality, tricky, multi-part adventure games.

Magnetic Moon

'Magnetic Moon' was Larry's first adventure, written originally for the Acorn and quickly converted to the Amstrad and Spectrum. It is the first in the 'Mike Erlin' series of games.

In this three-part adventure you start off aboard the Stellar Queen, the spaceship on which you, Mike Erline, serve. The Stellar Queen has been caught in what appears to be the magnetic attraction of an alien moon. Your captain, however, doesn't think that all is as it appears to be, so he sends down a search party to the planet below. Unfortunately, you're not on the team he selects for the job... so you decide to do a bit of freelancing and have a look yourself anyway. First, of course, you have to get off the ship without being stopped.

A tricky game because there's nothing to stop you from going down to the planet without having done everything you need to do on the spaceship first. You'll have to restart and play through the adventure again if you find you've forgotten to do something!

Starship Quest

As in the previous Mike Erlin game, you start aboard the spaceship Stellar Queen, and once again you want to return to the planet's surface. This time, though, you'll have to accomplish your escape before the ship goes into hyperspace – in about two minutes, which is not long to get all your equipment ready! Once on the planet you've got to try and discover the secret of the discs you obtained in the first adventure.

It's another massive, three-part game and a far better adventure, in my opinion, than Starship Quest, being a lot more friendly and better designed. Quite fun to play, though again it is probably too difficult for beginners.

The Axe of Kolt

Larry's third game concentrated on a new character: Alaric Blackmoon. Set in a fantasy world, it leaves the inky black void of space far behind for a more traditional hack'n'slash 'evil people can only be stopped by a magical object' fantasy scenario.

Your character, Alaric, is an out-of-work mercenary. Heck, you're so out of work that you've even had to sell your sword. Things start to look up, though, when you reach the town of Hengemire. It's there that you are recruited in the quest to find the Axe of Kolt which was buried with its last owner in his tomb. The reason that the axe is needed pretty sharpish is that the land is being overrun by evil lizard-men and only the axe can banish them forever! (Well, until the next game anyway).

Regarded as a true classic by many, 'The Axe of Kolt'

contains more action than Terminator 2, more puzzles than an episode of The Crystal Maze, more blood and guts than you'd see in Casualty and more silly names than you'd get in a Monty Python sketch. Highly recommended.

The Spectre of Castle Coris

After his promotion to Duke of High Jamack you'd think that Alaric Blackmoon would take time off to relax. But no, even a routine tour of his land turns into a brush with death in the form of the evil Spectre of Corwyn. It turns out that the Lizardmen are involved again together with a whole host of demons led by the dastardly sorcerer Zalazar.

Beginners might find themselves discouraged by the start of this adventure as it takes a lot of work to get into the main part of the game. Once you get past the initial hurdles, though, it is just as absorbing as the 'Axe of Kolt'. With two parts to work through there's plenty of adventure here to keep you busy for ages.

Scott Denyer / Delbert the Hamster

Adventure-writing student Scott Denyer juggled studying for his GCSEs and A-Levels with running his own homegrown software house, Delbert the Hamster. As well as his own games, he collaborated on titles with others and also re-released a bunch of Zodiac Software games.

Desmond and Gertrude

'Desmond and Gertrude' is a tale of two hearts kept apart by their families. One of the lovebirds is a princess, the other is a peasant. Your task is simple. You have to guide the two star-struck lovers to their secret rendezvous so that they can elope.

You can swop between the two lovers as you play through the game, so in effect you have two adventures in one. One part concerns the efforts of Desmond as he goes around his gutter of a home, but the most enjoyable section is the one involving Gertrude. She has to escape from her castle, making her way past the various security devices that her father has installed to keep her from her betrothed. The king wants Gertie to marry a very wet prince instead, so he's erected a huge green wall in the middle of the town.

The Gertrude half features some great puzzles but the game, although fun overall, is let down by the below-average section involving Desmond.

Brian and the Dishonest Politician

Arguably Scott's best game, you play Brian and you must stop the evil Garth Pitchfork from winning your local elections by standing against him. You have to gain the support of the people of your town by carrying out various tasks... a great excuse and justification for all the usual fetch quests that adventure games throw at you!

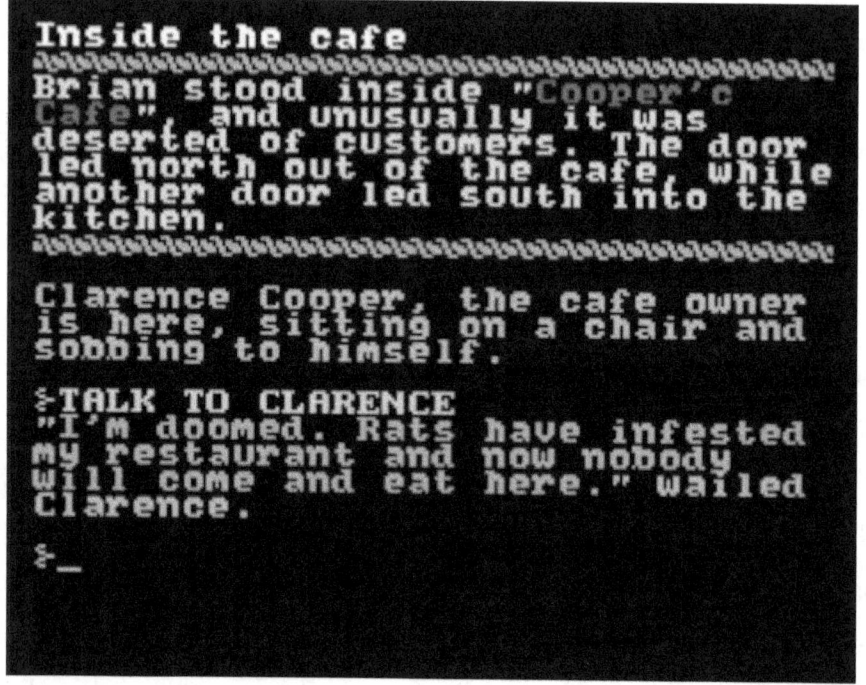

The game is a two-parter, with the second half being more of a traditional search/use adventure that lacks some of the charm and sparkle of the very original, first section.

Snow Joke!

A small, one location, game designed to fill the other side of a cassette tape. You start marooned in your car on a cold winter's day. The engine is dead, the doors are frozen and unless you get out and to shelter soon you're going to be in serious trouble.

You have to examine everything in sight, and quite a few things that aren't, if you want to get anywhere in this adventure.

Larry the Lemming's Urge for Extinction

In local legends, Lemmings have a biological urge to throw themselves off cliffs. Not exactly something that ensures a great chance of survival, which is why Larry the Lemming's mother has fitted him with an inflatable rubber ring and a parachute.

Playing Larry, your task is to kill yourself... but please, do it in a human manner! You'll need to remove the parachute and rubber ring first, of course.

A compact and tricky adventure with the author's usual humour and typically strange premise.

Other Adventures

Diablo!

Diablo! (with its free exclamation mark) by Mark Cantrell ranks up there with the likes of Kaptain Kook and Starship Quest, as one of the best sci-fi adventures ever written for the Spectrum. Its four player characters, OOPS, FOLLOW, RADIO and SAY TO commands (many of these features were previously unseen in a PAWed game) and its sheer attention to detail make it stand out from the crowd even in these enlightened times.

You control a four person team in their investigation of just what has happened on the spaceship Discovery... a seemingly abandoned ship, recently found floating in space. An easy task? Incidents at the start prove that it's not and with rumours that the devil's on board and trouble in the form of the mysterious character, Lawson, you'd better watch your (and the other characters) step.

The game comes in three jam-packed 128K parts which each form a 'deck' of the ship and assure value for money.

Diablo! Is a great little game. If you're a sci-fi fan, or an adventurer who likes a game with plenty to challenge you, you can't afford to miss this.

Jekyll and Hyde

Jekyll and Hyde, the award winning title by The Essential Myth, is a 3-part Spectrum 128K game that took me weeks of computer time to complete.

It's a Gothic tale in which you star as the mild-mannered Dr. Jekyll, in the midst of his great experiment. Most of the first part revolves around you making sure that the experiment goes ahead so that you turn into the evil Mr. Hyde.

The game is full of atmospheric text and although the map isn't huge, the puzzles are logical and quite well done with usually several ways of solving them. The first part is a simplistic affair, but by the time you get to the second and third parts you'll need all your wits about you. There's even a card game in Part Two which you must win, although I'll gladly admit that I did cheat on this by altering the basic routine which adds up your cash!

Part Three is very weird, especially near the end and very fast real-time movements (or yet more cheating) are needed in your quest to rid Jekyll of the abomination named Hyde.

Jekyll and Hyde is a game bursting with the indescribable 'it' factor. It's not huge and is not even that complex, when you really look at it, but it's such a hell of a good game that it'll have you playing it again and again.

A great game that should be on the shelves of any serious Spectrum adventurer.

Double Agent

Written without the aid of a commercial adventure writing system, Tom Frost's 'Double Agent' is a classic game which includes a novel twist – you play two characters, giving instructions to each in turn. Your task is to guide two agents around the planet Marego so that they can retrieve a valuable crystal. There's a lot of switching between the two characters in this split-screen game and you have to utilise their own special powers; one of the agents is very bright, the other is very strong but can't read a word of the Maregian language. An excellent little game from Tartan Software, that's well worth checking out.

The Gordello Incident

Continuing with Tom Frost's split-screen idea, utilised in Double Agent, you control two characters once again in Tartan's 'The Gordello Incident'. Basically this chap called Gordello has perfected the art of cloning humans. Well almost... he hasn't quite ironed out the kinks yet. You are a secret agent and Gordello has had the cheek to clone two copies of you. You're out to stop him from replacing world leaders with his clones and this ruling the world. The technical boys at the lab have devised a way of linking your brainwaves to those of the two clones that are in Gordello's clinic and it is those that you use to try and stop Gordello. There's only one small problem; these are sub-standard clones and so aren't quite up to scratch in the old mental department. One of the clones even does the opposite of whatever command you type in on the keyboard (e.g. GET KEY makes him drop the key, SOUTH makes him go north!). A good three-part game that's probably the hardest, most devious bit of interaction fiction that I've ever played.

Cloud 99

Written by one of my favourite adventure authors, Linda Wright, and originally published on her Marlin Games label, 'Cloud 99' also happens to be one of my favourite games. Old Jack Frost has been up to his tricks again and has messed about with the equipment in the weather-halls on Cloud 99. The whole world's weather is in turmoil and it's up to you to put right what Jack put wrong... but watch out, he's still about!

A wonderfully crafted adventure that kept me glued to my computer screen for days.

The Labours of Hercules

The famous Greek myth is really brought vividly to life in this huge and excellent game by Terry Taylor. You have to undertake the twelve labours in order that Hercules is allowed his freedom.

A wonderfully designed game with absolutely loads to do and a huge game map. There are several mazes included but each one is different and they're not so big that they're un-mappable. A very tricky title that should take you a while to finish.

The Hermitage

Written by Tony Collins, of Pegusus Software for his own The Guild software label, 'The Hermitage' is a gothic tale which places you in the habit of Ambrose, a monk who must seek out and destroy and evil hermit. That's in the first part of the game, anyway, the second part gives you the task of saving your soul from eternal damnation. 'The Hermitage' has a great atmosphere, spooky text and a layer of evil interwove into the descriptions.

Crack City

Written by Garry Cappuccini, this is a great game with possibly one of the most ambitious screen displays ever produced using the PAW system. Graphics of the locations and the characters are shown on-screen in this spy thriller. It's not just all about good looks. The puzzles haven't been neglected either, and although there isn't quite the amount of things to do as you'd expect in a more traditional text-only game, what's there is excellently thought out. Always fancied yourself as a bit of a James Bond? Well this game will let you have a go at the role, complete with gadgetry, evil villains, and lots of traps for you to fall into... but, amazingly, not many beautiful women to fall for. Oh well.

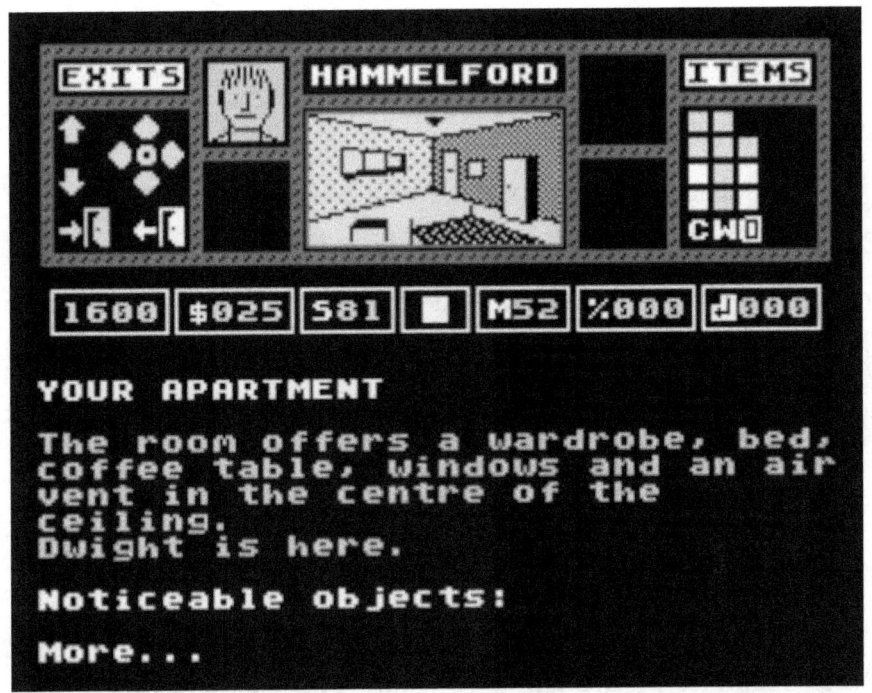

```
 EXITS       HAMMELFORD          ITEMS




                                     CW
```

```
 1600  $025  581    MS2  %000  J000
```

```
YOUR APARTMENT

The room offers a wardrobe, bed,
coffee table, windows and an air
vent in the centre of the
ceiling.
Dwight is here.

Noticeable objects:

More...
```

Captain Kook

Written by Paul Cardin, 'Captain Kook' is one of my favourite sci-fi adventures. It combines lots of tricky puzzles with a believable alien setting that is enhanced by Paul Cardin's sheet attention to detail. Even the poem that comes with the game is excellently written.

You play an alien cartographer, in this two-part PAWed game, that is in dire trouble. You awake from cryogenic suspension to find that your ship is on fire with its orbit rapidly decaying. As if that wasn't enough, the cryogenic unit has gone and retained vital parts of your memory!

Apart from fishing-themed adventure, 'The Inner Lakes', Captain Kook was the only game written and published by Paul on his The Silent Corner label.

The Book of the Dead

A cult classic, two-part GACed adventure written by The Essential Myth, the authors of 'Jekyll and Hyde'. You take on the role of an Egyptian godling and must manage to redeem your soul and take your rightful place among the gods. A classic adventure with moderate graphics and text, but devious problems and puzzles.

Theseus and the Minotaur

A two parter that'll be particularly of interest to fans of Greek legends. In the game you play Theseus, the illegitimate son of Aegeus (King of Athens). In part one you must find the sword and sandles hidden by Aegeus, in order to prove your birth-right.

In the second part the main task is to kill the Minotaur – a half man, half bull creature which feeds on human flesh and lives in the Labyrinth.

The game, by Anthony Collins, is well researched and great fun is to be had playing the part of Theseus.

Adventure Fanzines

ADVENTURE PROBE
NOVEMBER 1994   £2.00
VOLUME 8   ISSUE 11

Adventure Probe

Under the stewardships of editors Sandra Sharkey, Pat Winstanley, Mandy Rodrigues and Barbara Gibb, Adventure Probe was undoubtedly the glue holding the UK home-grown adventure community together.

Released on either a bi-monthly or monthly schedule, this A5 magazine (usually consisting of 50-60 photocopied pages), ran for an impressive twenty-one years between 1986 and 2007; at its height reaching over 500 subscribers.

Covering all 8-bit and 16-bit machines, and later PC gaming, the magazine featured news, reviews, articles, hints & tips, and an extremely lively letters section.

Adventure Probe spawned both its own software label and the long running 'The Adventurer's Convention' in the UK.

From Beyond

FROM BEYOND

Produced by Tim Kemp, who later helmed the Your Sinclair adventure pages, From Beyond was an A5 adventure fanzine that focussed on games for the ZX Spectrum range of computers.

Released on a bi-monthly schedule, the majority of reviews were written by Tim and his hand-picked team of contributors, giving the critical appraisals of games a very consistent and professional feel.

From Beyond was also the home of the Spectrum Public Domain Adventures library, for a time, taking on the collection of titles originally curated by Gordon Inglis of GI Games.

Red Herring

Arguably the most professionally produced UK adventure fanzine, Red Herring was put together by editors Marion Taylor and adventure author Sue Medley (who also edited the SynTax disk-based magazine).

Spiral-bound and printed on stiff paper, with an impeccably produced layout, the magazine was enhanced by artwork from

Marion's husband, cartoonist Ken Taylor.

Reaching over 250 subscribers and spanning sixteen issues between 1991 and 1994, Red Herring covered a good mix of 8-bit, 16-bit and PC adventures and sometimes strayed into other areas such as strategy games and Play By Mail.

The Beginner's Guide to Adventures

1. What is an adventure game?

An adventure is like an interactive book where *you* take the part of the main character and must accomplish a series of tasks in a world inside your computer. Jobs need to be completed and puzzles solved before you have finished the game.

Your computer is your guide in this world. It acts as your senses and changes the world in response to commands typed in simple, abbreviated sentences on the keyboard.

2. Moving around

It's all very well having this computer created world but how do you move around in it? Most adventures use the eight points of the compass to indicate direction and also up and down. These are normally abbreviated to the first letter e.g. N might send you to the North, or NE to the North East.

Most adventures print up your visible exits on the screen but this doesn't normally include secret exits. You'll have to find those yourself!

Also GO is sometimes used to go through places. You can often GO DOOR if there is one or GO CAFÉ to get into a café. Similarly EXIT, OUT AND ENTER can often be used.

3. Actions

Most actions can be performed by a simple VERB-NOUN input. For instance, if you want to take a pen you've seen lying around type GET PEN or TAKE PEN. To jump into a lake, type JUMP LAKE. To eat some food, type EAT FOOD.

You can often get everything in a location by typing GET ALL. Some programs get complicated and allow you to GET ALL FROM THE BOX EXCEPT THE PUDDING. Sometimes you can use punctuation to link commands together for example: JUMP LAKE, GO NORTH, TAKE SWORD.

4. Other Commands

LOOK or REDESCRIBE (usually abbreviated to L or R) – Repeats the description of your current location in the world. Sometimes it's necessary to do this to notice something that has changed.

INVENTORY (I) – Gives you a list of the items that you are carrying and wearing.

EXAMINE (sometimes abbreviated as X) – This allows you to look more closely at an object or piece of scenery. E.g. EXAMINE CHEST. Looking in containers, such as chests or drawers, may reveal their contents or you may have to SEARCH them; once, twice or multiple times!

SAVE – LOAD – Allows you to save or load a game position to and from cassette or disk. RS and RL (shortened from RAMSAVE and RAMLOAD) can sometimes be used to temporarily make a copy of your progress on the internal memory of your computer. Remember that you'll use this progress when you turn your computer off!

HELP – Sometimes gives you hints or suggestions on how to progress.

QUIT – Allows you to quit the game and restart.

5. Hints and Tips

Here are some general tips for successful adventuring.

- Make a map, showing objects, exits and special points that a location have.
- Read everything carefully, or else you may miss something important.
- Examine and search everything carefully, several times. Sometimes you may need to LOOK UNDER, BEHIND or INside objects.
- If you can't get across what you want the computer to do, try rephrasing your commands. For example, if GO CAR doesn't work, try GET IN CAR, CLIMB INTO CAR, ENTER CAR or DRIVE CAR. Perhaps you just need to OPEN or UNLOCK the car DOOR first!
- SAVE your game regularly, in case you die, and keep a whole set of saved positions on tape to go back to.
- And lastly, experiment. As long as you've saved your game you won't lose out.

Index

www.ingramcontent.com/pod-product-compliance
Lightning Source LLC
Chambersburg PA
CBHW071419180526
45170CB00001B/152